personal **&** powerful

personal & powerful

In a world
where we can
stand in a crowd
and feel
alone,
do you feel
known, heard,
understood and
met?

written by

Willow Weston

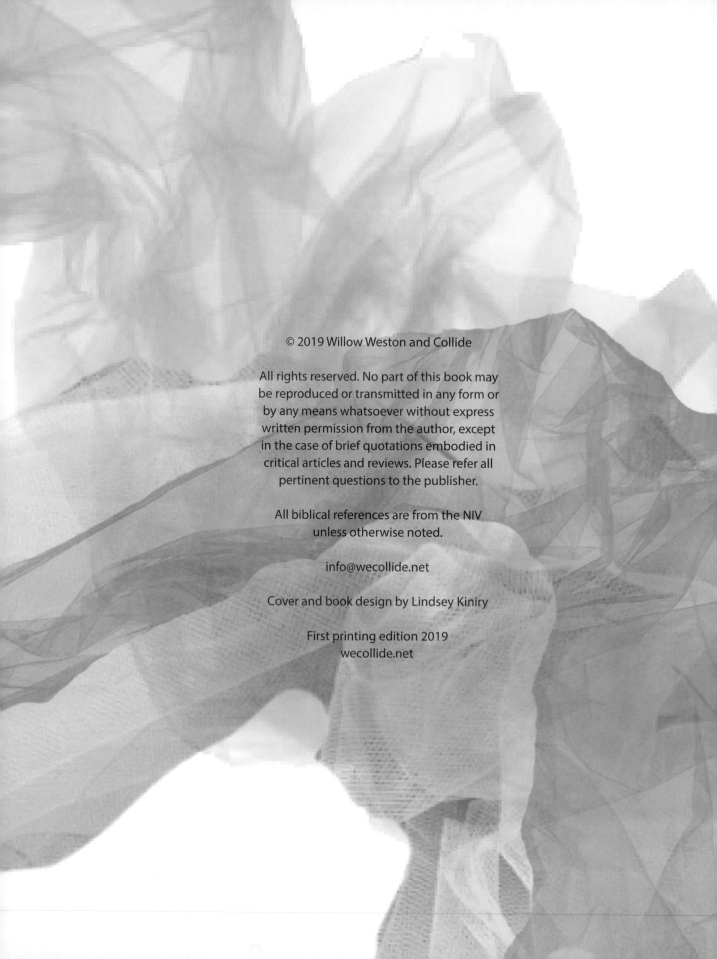

All biblical references are from the NIV
unless otherwise noted.

info@wecollide.net

Cover and book design by Lindsey Kiniry

First printing edition 2019
wecollide.net

Table of Contents

The Collide Story

I remember walking into a counseling office over a decade ago because my pain was chasing me down. I had run into Jesus and had even been leading in ministry for years prior to walking in for help, but God was inviting me into a deeper healing than I had yet to receive and perhaps a higher calling than I had yet to understand. I walked in for guidance because my pain was leaking out in ways that scared me. I sat in that counselor's office and stared at her clock as she asked me the all too expected question: "So what brings you in here today?"

I had a run-in with Jesus Christ in that office that had nothing to do with the counselor. God gave me two words: wounded collision. He helped me to see that I was born into pain. I had collided with wounds that were never healed, and they wounded me and now I wounded others. Sometimes it seems like we are all bumping around, colliding and wounding each other. I sat in that room desperate for all of us to have a new kind of collision. My pain was crying out for it.

When I see Jesus, He collides with people and rather than wounding them, He leaves them more whole. God's Spirit showed up in that counseling office in a way that pierced the air. God invited me to see those who wounded me from His perspective rather than my own. God called me to enter people's brokenness, instead of running from it. God reminded me that He is, indeed, a God who wipes brokenness all over Himself. I was being invited to collide with Jesus in my brokenness and invite others to come along.

So, I walked out of that appointment holding a spiritual concept, but even more, I knew in my innards that I was being called to do something big with those two words. Soon afterwards a beautiful young college aged girl from church asked if I would mentor her. I wasn't feelin' like the mentoring type right about then. She said she wanted to learn more about Jesus. I invited her to get together and study the Bible and see what happens when Jesus collides with wounded people. She was excited, so excited, that she invited all her friends, because twenty-some college women came knocking on my door.

We spent the next several years looking at Jesus colliding with people in the New Testament and as we did, He collided with us too. When Jesus restored the shriveled man's hand, He too, restored these college girls' shriveled self-esteems. When Jesus said to the woman caught in the act of adultery, "Go and sin no more", He too, said this to the young woman in my living room who had been caught stark naked in shame and Jesus set her free. When Jesus went out of His way to collide with the woman at the well who was going from man to man to man because she was so thirsty, Jesus too, met the college girls in my living room and He gave them something to drink that quenched their parched living. Those twenty girls and I experienced a new kind of collision when we ran into Jesus, one that brought about wholeness.

Most of the girls graduated and moved away from college. There were four girls left and they wanted to keep meeting. I prayed, and God said, "I am not into us 4 and no more Bible studies, it's time they teach the message." I was working as a college minister at the time and this idea came out of nowhere. I had a lot of other things on my plate, not to mention a full-time job, a husband and two kids. God handed us an opportunity to do something to impact lives that was beyond our understanding, but we had to act on His invitation. So, we did an experiment and that experiment led to what is now Collide, this ministry, that invites women of all ages, races, socioeconomic statuses, faith backgrounds, and life places to run into Jesus and as they do, they are forever transformed.

God took a story of pain and brokenness and turned it into this beautiful ministry we call Collide. We shape and craft events, conferences and retreats for thousands of women every year. We now have a counseling program assisting people who desire to walk towards healing in their life. We encourage and support mentoring, where women meet in life changing intergenerational relationships and co-learn from one another. We have a blog that God is using to invite people all around the country to collide with Jesus. We have a podcast which encourages women weekly with engaging content that is reflective of Jesus' love for them. We have a leadership and ministry development program where we are inviting women to tap into God's purpose for their lives. We have a church bridging program partnering with many local churches in the hopes of inviting women to walk a bridge from our events into the local church, so they will keep colliding. We have an amazing staff of gifted passionate, fierce women who are giving their lives away for this mission. And in 2018, we launched our Bible studies which we are creating and sharing in the hopes that more and more people will run into Christ.

I am continually amazed by this Jesus who shows up right smack dab in the midst of our mess and pain and walks us into healing and purpose. Collide has become a place, a community, a movement for so many to run into Jesus just as they are. My hope is that in the same way God met me years ago when I most needed it, He too will meet you right where you find yourself. He is a God who collides... so get ready because He does incredible, big, mighty, miraculous, unimaginable things when you run into Him.

Willow Weston
founder and director of Collide

Collide Values

We value women colliding with Jesus and His teachings.

We value and encourage authenticity (telling our story as it really is).

We value recognizing brokenness, so it can be made whole.

We value the experience and support that comes from an intergenerational community of women of all ages, church backgrounds, life experiences, and faith stages.

We value teaching a theology that runs into the holistic parts of who we are, to encourage a healthy spirituality.

We value pushing towards growth and next steps to go further on one's journey with God.

We value challenging, equipping and inspiring people to serve, lead, minister and use their gifts in order to live into their God-given purpose and change lives.

Collide invites people of all ages, stages, experiences and faith backgrounds, as imperfect or broken as they may be on their journey, to authentically run into Jesus; as He collides with them, they are forever transformed.

Collide Mission

Who we are and who we aren't

We are everyday chicks running into Jesus. This Bible study was written, researched and created by ordinary women of all ages, stages and backgrounds, desiring to know God. We have indigestion, PMS, anxiety, and bad hair days. We work jobs, serve on PTA boards, sit on church committees, coach sports and attempt to bless our neighbors. We have different skin colors, different generational experiences, different faith backgrounds and different economic statuses. We like Cheetos and red wine, candles, a good book and a walk on the beach. We get insecure and let fear get in our way sometimes. We battle and wrestle and pray and pray. We have bills to pay, kids to raise, relationships to reconcile and big dreams we'd like to see become reality. We are your neighbors, your friends, your everyday women.

We are not Bible scholars. We have not been to Seminary. We don't have a lot of letters after our name. We don't speak Hebrew or Greek. We are not all that impressive in "religious" circles. If you are looking for that kind of Bible study resource, there are so many great ones, and this might not be the one for you. We merely desire God and are mesmerized by Jesus. We want to learn, grow, study and be challenged and inspired by who God is and who He calls us to be. It is this desire that has led us to run into Jesus and to invite others to come along.

We are still in the midst of our story. We are in chapter 6, not at the end of the book. We have not "arrived." God's not done with us. What we think, feel, or believe might transform, morph, or reconstruct as God continues to collide with us. Who we are now and who we are becoming leaves room for us to be in process, to seek, to ask questions and to be God's kids. We believe God is the best Author and He writes the best story and the story that He is writing in your life and ours is being written as we speak… and so we engage His best story and trust Him for chapter 8, chapter 9 and so on.

We don't have all the answers. We did not set out to write Bible studies because we think we have the Holy Bible nailed down. We do not think we know the answers to all the questions. We don't think we can solve age-old theological debates nor current hot button arguments. We don't think we are tighter with the Big Man upstairs and therefore can tell you all that you need to know. All we know for sure is that God is alive and well. He loves us, and He shows just how much He loves us in Jesus Christ. We know for sure that God desires to collide with us and when we do we are forever transformed. Because we don't have all the answers, we are okay with inviting you, our friends, to come with us as we collide with Jesus together. We don't feel the pressure to be know-it-alls, experts or professional "Christians". Neither do we feel we need to provide you with all the answers, easy answers, formulas or a specified spiritual "track" that someone else prescribes. Let's together read, reflect, ruminate and respond. Let's not be afraid to have questions that lack easy answers. Let's not think God isn't big enough to handle our doubt. Let's not limit God to our confusion and misunderstandings. Let's not box Him in either. Let's just collide with Jesus and see what He will do.

We are broken. We have been abused, used, betrayed, judged, manipulated, beat down and lied to. We have skeletons in the closet, a long list of mistakes, shady pasts, paralytic fear and deep-seated bitterness we struggle with. We will not pretend we are someone we aren't, and we won't ask you to either. We are not put together. We are not perfect. We are not immortal. We are not finished, faultless or foolproof. We are not Christian poster children. We are sojourners, inviting you, in your brokenness, to walk alongside us in ours, and together, we will collide with Jesus and by His wounds, we will be made whole.

We aren't afraid to engage our brokenness or yours. We no longer want our past to determine our present. We know that the pain we have experienced can easily walk into all of our collisions and we want more than that for our lives. We want to see our wounds find their Healer. We want to see our pain experience redemption. We want to see our brokenness be used for good. We know there's no other way around pain than to allow Jesus to meet us in it. So, we let Him. We sit in discomfort, we remember, we grieve, we cry, we forgive, we get angry and cry out like the Psalmist. But we don't avoid, ignore or devalue our pain or yours. We believe God meets us where we are. We don't believe you have to get it together before God will run into your life. It is actually in the midst of pain and brokenness that God does His greatest work.

We have big hopes. We believe that this project, to create content that invites people to collide with Jesus, has the potential to change your life and your friends' lives and your neighbors and on and on. We believe this because when people collide with Jesus they are never the same. We see this all the time in our ministry. When people run into who God is, they become who they are made to be. We have big God-sized dreams that when we together, collide with Jesus, we will be changed and then we together can change the world.

How to use this study

We hand crafted this study for women just like you. It has been designed to be used in the way that works best, personally, for wherever you find yourself. We know that women experience a variety of different roles, seasons, and circumstances. We encourage you to engage this study with your morning cup o' coffee, to pull it out of your handbag while you wait for your kids to be done with soccer practice. Grab it off the shelf when you are struggling to find purpose or invite some friends over and do it together. Jesus meets you along the way, so as you journey, doing whatever it is you do, may you enjoy colliding with Him.

We fashioned this study with freedom and joy in mind. Our hope is that colliding with Jesus brings gratification and not guilt, life and not condemnation, power and not oppression. So please be a friend to yourself and enter into this study with freedom knowing God invites you to come and collide with Him, not so He can critique you or grade you, but so He can love and spend time with you. God doesn't have an expectation of the number of pages you must read or a time-line of how fast you must complete this study. God won't be mad at you if you leave some reflection questions blank or even if you think a question we ask is dumb. It probably is. God merely wants to be with you. Enjoy your time with Him.

We constructed this study with a few simple prompts to invite your engagement.

Read

We will invite you to read a passage of Scripture that unfolds a collision with Jesus and corresponding Scripture that applies. Our desire is that as you see Jesus collide with others, you will also experience this living God collide with you.

Reflect

Our hope is that you would not just read or "know facts" about the Bible, but instead that you would allow your heart and mind to go to deeper places: to reflect, to think, to mull, to consider. It is in our reflection that God can have some of His greatest conversations with each one of us. And it is in these conversations that transformation, guidance, wisdom and healing take place. We have intentionally written questions that will invite you to purposely reflect so that you can experience just that.

Ruminate

There will be points where we will encourage you to stop and chew, wrestle, learn or meditate on more. This is where ruminating on thoughts, Scripture, and quotes will bless you and invite you further into a collision with Jesus.

Respond

You can't stay the same and go with God. Every time Jesus collides with people they are forever transformed. He often calls us to take action, to pray, to move, to serve, to give, to lay down, to surrender, to not merely be "hearers" of the word but "doers". Our hope is that we will not just "study" God, but that we will become people who respond to our collisions with Jesus in a way that helps us see transformation in our own lives, that then leads to transformation in the lives of those around us.

Leader Guide

When we study God's word together, we hear multiple perspectives which help enhance our experience. If you would like to lead a group of women through this study, we have created a Leader Guide which you will find at the end of this book. Our hope is that this guide will help you lead your group into meaningful conversation as you support and encourage one another.

Let's collide . . .

Surrounded Yet All Alone

personal &
powerful

If there's one thing I've learned about crowds, it's that you can be surrounded and feel completely alone. This can be true in a stadium or a theater, at a sporting event, in your own family, at school, work, and even right now, wherever you find yourself. You can feel like no one sees you, no one gets you, and no one truly knows you. You're just another number.

ENTERTAINMENT PRESENTS 123 Crowded Avenue, Judgyville		
LAST NAME **WESTON,**		FIRST NAME **WILLOW**
SECTION 148	ROW F	SEAT 12
no one sees you, no one gets you, and no one truly knows you yourejustanothernumber.com		

If you look around a room or a gathering, it's easy to see the crowd and not the person. It's easy to see what's on the surface. It's easy to make assumptions, to sum each other up and to see what we don't have in common rather than what we do. I think we do that a lot as women. I think we look at each other and we do that thing…

I'm a working mom… she's a stay at home mom.
She's got beautiful curly hair… I've got stick straight hair.
I wear sweats… she looks like she just stepped out of a Nordstrom catalog.
She breastfeeds… I bottle feed.
She can eat anything she wants… I gain weight looking at a bagel.
I'm tired… she's superwoman.
She's adventurous… I go to Costco.
I quit most things I start… she volunteers for everything.
She has a jillion followers… I barely get any likes.
I Pin things… she originates them.
She's got everything a girl could ever dream to have… I have every dream a girl could long for but don't have.

Reflect

How do you see women comparing themselves to each other?

I...	She...

Rather than see what we have in common, we so often create space between ourselves and other women by stacking up our differences. What do you think we as women have in common?

As women we have had to be brave. As women we have had to endure things no one should ever have to endure. We have persevered. We have fought and we are strong. What I've seen time and time again at Collide conferences is that hundreds of us gather, but in every chair is a story. And if we had all the time in the world to share our stories with one another, we would be blown away by the commonalities we share rather than the differences.

In the same room, we have women who have dreamed to be moms and over and over again, their dreams keep getting dashed, alongside women who have lost the love of their lives and the pain is just too much. In the same room we have women who have been sexually assaulted and the silence is killing them alongside women who've given up on the church because the church gave up on them. In the same room we have women who aren't sure forgiveness is an option for them because they feel so ashamed about what they've done alongside women who are grieving their spouse, or fighting cancer, or bravely showing up to life every day in spite of the suicidal thoughts that scream at them not to.

Look around at the women you're surrounded by: your sisters, moms, aunts, friends, coworkers, neighbors, acquaintances, and enemies. Every woman has a story and what we have in common is that we can all resonate with pain and hardship and facing circumstances we feel helpless to change. Yet we hold the deep desire to see transformation, movement forward, and motion towards getting unstuck. And in the midst of that, we can often feel alone, forgetting that other women feel the exact same way.

I was walking out of a coffee shop last year that three women were walking into. I waited while they filed in and then one sweetly held the door for me to walk out before she could walk in. She said, "Willow Weston." I didn't recognize her but smiled, wondering if I heard her right in saying my name. I didn't know her name so it caught me off guard. I smiled as we passed by each other. Maybe she sensed my hesitation that was caused by not being able to reply in the same familiar way. Then she said to her friends, "Everyone knows Willow Weston." This woman was kind and friendly and even opened the door for me. Her intention was to compliment. She assumes a lot of people know me in our town, but what she doesn't know is… I walked out and got into my car and started crying.

You can feel surrounded by people and yet feel all alone.
It doesn't matter how big or tight your family is, it doesn't matter how many followers you have on Insta, it doesn't matter how great your friendship group proves to be, it doesn't matter how many kids are in your nest, it doesn't matter what size stage you stand on, it doesn't matter how many gatherings you get invited to. You can feel alone while being completely surrounded.

The collision we are centering our conversation around in this Bible study is out of **Mark 5:21-43**. It is an incredible passage about two females whose stories unexpectedly collide and their lives share commonalities; perhaps they wished they didn't. The story starts out in a crowd...

Read

²¹When Jesus had again crossed over by boat to the other side of the lake, a large crowd gathered around him while he was by the lake. ²²Then one of the synagogue leaders, named Jairus, came, and when he saw Jesus, he fell at his feet. ²³He pleaded earnestly with him, "My little daughter is dying. Please come and put your hands on her so that she will be healed and live." ²⁴So Jesus went with him. A large crowd followed and pressed around him. ²⁵And a woman was there who had been subject to bleeding for twelve years. ²⁶She had suffered a great deal under the care of many doctors and had spent all she had, yet instead of getting better she grew worse. **Mark 5:21-26**

Reflect

This woman stood in a crowd with Jesus and Jesus' groupies and a desperate dad hoping for a miracle. How do you think the bleeding woman felt standing in this crowd?

Recently, I was walking on a trail with my friend Kara and we ran into a guy who was higher than a kite. He was surrounded by his belongings in a forest and was trippin' pretty hardcore. We kept walking and on our way back, we saw the same man further down the trail lying with his face pressed into the gravel. He wasn't moving. As soon as we spotted him, a group of maybe twenty high school cross country runners and their coaches passed us. And they passed him too.

Every one of them.

They had to veer to the left to run by his body instead of over it. And without skipping a beat, they did. To the coach's credit, he came running back and stood over the man asking if he wanted help and thank God, he was alive but struggled to groan a "no" and stayed lying there. So the coach ran off to catch up to his kids who were long gone. Kara and I couldn't just leave this man for dead. We called 911 and had to wait for quite awhile and while we did, you know what we saw? We saw person after person passing by this man.

Surrounded yet all alone.

I sat in a room full of women on our Volunteer Ministry Team who were each taking turns vulnerably sharing with each other. One of the smartest, kindest, most beautiful young women you could ever meet piped up. And you have to know when you hear this story that she has an amazing family she is close with, a tight group of friends and roommates she does life alongside. She shines as a leader in college and in her church. The previous summer she was excited to enter into the field of work she had been studying so hard for, but she experienced rejection after rejection. Everything she had put her hope in wasn't working out. She said that she got to a point where she didn't want to be here anymore. Here she was telling us this, months later, and no one else in her life knew either.

Reflect

How is it that an amazing, beautiful, smart, talented woman enveloped by friends and family gets this down and discouraged without anyone ever knowing?

Surrounded yet all alone.

I sat with a mom recently. She did that whole "just pray for me but I'm not going to say why" thing. Instead of talking or praying, I looked at her. I saw her eyes. She saw mine. That's all it took. Next thing you know, she became tearful while doing that "I'm sorry I'm crying" thing. Then she busted out in story as though she'd been holding it in far too long. She said she didn't want to tell anyone what was going on because it wasn't her story to tell. It was her kid's story. I've heard that line before from the woman covering for her husband's reputation, and from the friend covering for someone else's secret, and from the daughter covering for her dad's screw up, and from the victim covering for someone else's assault. Here this mom sat, undone, and though it had become her story too, she would protect another at her own expense.

Surrounded yet all alone.

How can we be surrounded and yet feel alone? There are many reasons why we can feel this way. See which ways below resonate with you or people you do life with.

- **We can feel alone because our circumstances look so different than those around us.** When you get invited to babysit on Valentine's Day because you're single so that your married friends can go out, your aloneness feels magnified. When you don't get invited to things because you can't afford it and they can, you not only feel isolated, you also feel broke. When you don't get invited to mimosas with the moms because you aren't one, it reminds you that you're left out and highlights why. When they all gather but leave you off the list because your husband fights fires, fights wars or fights layovers, it's easy to feel forgotten. There are so many circumstances that just plain create feelings of loneliness.

- **We can feel alone because we find ourselves in a season that leaves no room for relationship.** Some of us are in a season of being overwhelmed, overworked, overstressed, overcommitted, so we find ourselves under capacity, under available, under involved, and under connected.

- **We can feel alone because we assume we are the only one.** We often think we are the only one who's grieving our teenagers, the only one whose marriage is hard, the only one who fears her diagnosis, the only one who is angry, the only one who knows this pain, the only one whose past sneaks up on her present.

- **We can feel alone because we are too ashamed to let others in.** When we declare bankruptcy, we hope no one reads the paper. When we lie a thousand times, it was all to hide the one lie that was trying to hide the one truth that we wish wasn't true. When we've blown it, when we've been living a double life, when we've been unfaithful, when we've fallen off the wagon, it's then that we go unescorted. Because who wants to be like, "Hey, want to come and sit in my shame?" So we sit in it alone.

- **We can feel alone because we don't want to change, so we don't let people know what needs changing.** If you don't want to change your eating disorder, you won't tell people you have one. If you don't want to experience an intervention, you won't hint it's needed. If you don't want to hear people tell you to rest, you won't let on to how exhausted you really are.

We can feel alone because we don't want to burden others so we pack this giant heavy load ourselves. Our load is so messy or confusing or full of doubt that we don't want to get it on others. It's too much to bear to hand off, so we walk around weighed down trying to carry it by ourselves.

We can feel alone because we believe asking for help or reaching out for someone to walk alongside us is weak. We can assume that we should be able to pull ourselves up by the bootstraps, figure it out on our own, and work harder. We can view asking God and others for help as a sign of pure weakness that points to our inability to manage, problem solve, cope, and self lead. We think reaching out and inviting others in will damage our credibility, reputation and self image so we'd rather be alone and have others think we are something we aren't.

Reflect

Go back through the various reasons we often feel alone and circle the ones you resonate with most. Take some time to write below the top 2-3 reasons you often find you feel alone and why you think you do.

I sat down with the young woman I mentioned earlier, who had gotten to a place where she didn't want to be here anymore. I straight up asked her, how she could be in that kind of place and not invite anyone in. She started telling me about her grandfather's funeral. She loved him very much. The whole family did. They took up a whole row in the front of the church. This young woman sat there crying her eyes out grieving. She looked down the row at her grandmother, the matriarch of the family. Her grandmother was poised, calm, unmoved, without emotion. This young woman said, "My grandmother was strong for everyone and I guess when I think of strength, I think of my grandma." Perhaps she was leading herself there, but I suggested to her what I am also going to suggest to us, "Perhaps you should redefine strength."

Respond

As we close up part one of this study, pray this prayer along with me by reading it aloud or to yourself...

God, sometimes I feel alone. I know you promise that you surround me and yet I don't often feel it or believe it. I pray that where I find my circumstances and my thoughts convincing me I am on my own, God, help me to see you are with me. If I have been creating my own loneliness, help me to no longer do that. Help me to reach out to you and to others. Surround my life with community, help, friendship and presence. Jesus, will you collide with me in the place I now find myself and bring about all that I need? Amen.

Redefining Strength 2

personal &
powerful

We need to *redefine strength* because *if strength keeps you locked up in closets,* if strength has you *second guessing* grace, if strength *keeps you stuck,* if strength has you *hiding the truth,* if strength means you *don't* feel and you *don't* emote, if strength means you'll *sit in darkness* rather than *come into the light,* if *strength means* you have to be fake, if *strength means you have* to swim in shame, if strength means there is no *forgiveness* nor asking for it, if *strength means* you can't tell your story, if strength means *you run solo,* if strength means *you have to fight all your battles* on your own, if strength means *you can't ask for help,*

then what is our strength doing for us?!

Reflect

How do you see women defining strength in ways that are not helpful?

How have you personally mis-defined strength?

Do any of your definitions keep you lonely, isolated, silent or stuck, not getting the help you need?

Read

[21]When Jesus had again crossed over by boat to the other side of the lake, a large crowd gathered around him while he was by the lake. [22]Then one of the synagogue leaders, named Jairus, came, and when he saw Jesus, he fell at his feet. [23]He pleaded earnestly with him, "My little daughter is dying. Please come and put your hands on her so that she will be healed and live." [24]So Jesus went with him. **Mark 5:21-24a**

The entire story starts out with Jesus hopping off a boat and being immediately surrounded by a crowd. Word had already spread that Jesus just gave cards back to a guy who hadn't been playing with a full deck in a long time. That'll draw some looky loos. It was in this kind of scene that we see an important and respected religious leader, Jairus, come to collide with Jesus.[1] This religious leader and his religious friends would have most likely had a real issue with Jesus because they had other ideas as to what God coming into the world would look like. And I mean, I bet a lot of us can resonate, like, "What? God on a boat? Riding donkeys, rollin' into weddings making wine, forgiving get-around girls and hanging out with guys who lop people's ears off?" They would've seen Jesus as threatening their orthodoxy, their politics, and the religious system they created to benefit themselves. They were a people looking for God but saw Jesus as getting in God's way.

Sometimes what we want to see most is standing right in front of us but we miss it because it looks different than we expected it to.

This religious leader was a big deal, but there was something about Jesus that seemed to Jairus like a bigger deal because he put down his title, his pride, his expectations, his prejudice and his definition of strength and came falling at Jesus' feet pleading, "My little daughter is dying. Please come and put your hands on her so that she will be healed and live."

Sometimes what we want to see most is standing *right in front of us* but we miss it because it looks different than we expected it to.

Barclay, W. (2001). *The New Daily Study Bible: The Gospel of Mark* (pp. 145–146). Edinburgh: Saint Andrew Press.

Reflect

How do you think a typical religious leader like Jairus would have defined strength?

What did Jairus risk in coming to Jesus in a crowd and begging for help?

If you were this man and your daughter was dying, what lengths would you go to for her?

What did his request require him to hope about Jesus?

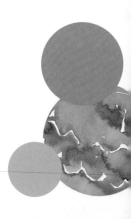

As we all know, life has a way of reminding us just how powerless we are. You might be called boss at work, but that doesn't mean you have the power to boss cancer around. You might be called wealthy by your financial advisors, but your wealth doesn't have the power to buy your peace. You might be called a power lifter at the gym, but you don't actually have the power to lift the heavy weight that burdens you. This man had a lot of power but he didn't have the power to save his daughter. And we can resonate.

Ruminate

Read the following passages and answer the questions attached:

Ask and it will be given to you; seek and you will find; knock and the door will be opened to you. **Matthew 7:7**

According to this verse, when will "it be given to you"?

Let us then approach God's throne of grace with confidence, so that we may receive mercy and find grace to help us in our time of need. **Hebrews 4:16**

According to Hebrews 4:16, when do you receive mercy and find grace?

²⁸Then they cried out to the Lord in their trouble, and he brought them out of their distress. ²⁹He stilled the storm to a whisper; the waves of the sea were hushed. ³⁰They were glad when it grew calm, and he guided them to their desired haven. **Psalm 107:28-30**

When did the Lord bring them out of their distress?

*Jesus answered her, "If you knew the gift of God and who it is that asks you for a drink, you would have asked him and he would have given you living water." **John 4:10***

When did Jesus suggest to the woman that she would experience the living water that truly satisfies?

*¹⁸Yet the Lord longs to be gracious to you; therefore he will rise up to show you compassion. For the Lord is a God of justice. Blessed are all who wait for him! ¹⁹People of Zion, who live in Jerusalem, you will weep no more. How gracious he will be when you cry for help! As soon as he hears, he will answer you. **Isaiah 30:18-19***

When did the Lord show His love and compassion?

So often we think if we are truly strong, then we don't need God and we shouldn't need others. We think we need to sit in our stuff alone. We need to keep our mistakes to ourselves. We need to hope for a miracle, but not utter that hope aloud. We need to remain silent with our grief. We need to keep our anxiety secret. Being alone in our mess, mistakes, hopes, grief and anxiety does nothing for us. In fact, Scripture seems to show that when we ask, when we draw near, when we cry out, that's when we receive what we need most.

"Some people think God does not like to be troubled with our constant coming and asking. The way to trouble God is not to come at all." ~ Dwight L. Moody

Dwight L. Moody says, "Some people think God does not like to be troubled with our constant coming and asking. The way to trouble God is not to come at all."[2] I agree. Weakness to us looks like strength to God. Crying in grief looks like strength to trust you can be with God as you are. Confession of sins looks like strength to risk God has the power to make what is scarlet, white as snow. Being vulnerable, sharing your fears in community looks like strength to hope that God brings us help through His people. It's when we put aside our false ideas of what strength looks like and we come to Jesus risking looking weak, that we tap into our most courageous selves. This man, Jairus, did just that. He came needing what he knew only Jesus had.

This collision between Jairus and Jesus fiercely challenges our definition of strength. Spoiler alert: it was because this strong, successful, independent, leader risked looking weak, and redefined strength, that he ended up seeing his daughter's life saved. What if he would have stayed home because that's what strong people do? Strong people keep to themselves. Strong people tell no one. Strong people handle what comes their way. Strong people ride the storm.

Reflect

Spend some time redefining strength. Instead of how we often define strength, fill in the blanks below, defining strength in a way that invites relationship, community, support, help, and presence.

Strong people...recognize when they need help and ask for it.

Strong people…

Strong people…

Strong people…

the Bible describes Jesus' response to Jairus'
request for help by saying, *"So Jesus went with him."* I love
that. I love that Jesus wasn't like, "Let me look at my Google
calendar. Oh bummer, I have a 1 o'clock. Plus you and your
people haven't given me the time of day." Nope, Jesus went
with him. And He goes with us too.

Reflect

In what ways could Jesus have responded to this man?

What do you love about Jesus' response?

Respond

Pray:

Jesus, I love that your response to this man who needed help was to go with him. Will you go with me? Will you go with me in the ways I need help and guidance? Will you go with me to the places that hurt and cry out for a healing? Will you go with me to my loved ones that need a miracle? Redefine strength in my life. Help me to see reaching out and drawing near as the way I tap into your ultimate strength and power and let me be okay doing so. God, I have places in my life that need you and my strength isn't strong enough to change the things that need changing. I need you to be my Strength and my Savior. I hand you my life and every part of it. Lord, collide with me here and be strong where I am not. Amen.

Impersonal and Weak 3

personal &
powerful

Read

²⁴...A large crowd followed and pressed around him. ²⁵And a woman was there who had been subject to bleeding for twelve years. ²⁶She had suffered a great deal under the care of many doctors and had spent all she had, yet instead of getting better she grew worse. **Mark 5:24-26**

The Old Testament passage in **Leviticus 15:25-27** describes her "unclean" state in this culture because of her bleeding: *²⁵When a woman has a discharge of blood for many days at a time other than her monthly period or has a discharge that continues beyond her period, she will be unclean as long as she has the discharge, just as in the days of her period. ²⁶Any bed she lies on while her discharge continues will be unclean, as is her bed during her monthly period, and anything she sits on will be unclean, as during her period. ²⁷Anyone who touches them will be unclean; they must wash their clothes and bathe with water, and they will be unclean till evening.*

Ruminate

Some things to know about being unclean:

- **There were many reasons one could be considered unclean:** "Some bodily discharges also make people unclean. Mothers are polluted by the puerperal discharge for forty days after giving birth to a son, and for eighty days after bearing a daughter (Lv. 12). Sexual intercourse pollutes both parties for a day and menstruation makes a woman unclean for a week (Lv. 15:18–19). Long-term discharges from the sexual organs make people unclean for as long as the discharge continues. Skin diseases of various sorts may also make a person unclean... Anyone suffering from a polluting skin condition remains unclean until it clears up. In general, short-term human uncleanness may be cleared by waiting a day and washing in water. When a condition causing long-term uncleanness clears up (e.g. skin disease), the sufferer has also to offer a sacrifice so as to become ritually clean again (Lv. 14)."[3]

3 Wenham, G. J. (1996). Clean and Unclean. In D. R. W. Wood, I. H. Marshall, A. R. Millard, J. I. Packer, & D. J. Wiseman (Eds.), New Bible dictionary (3rd ed., p. 210). Leicester, England; Downers Grove, IL: InterVarsity Press.

Being considered unclean led to banishment. The following describes just how banished one with a skin disease would be: "Any such skin disease rendered the sufferer unclean. He was banished from the fellowship of men; he must dwell alone outside the camp; he must go with rent clothes, bared head, a covering upon his upper lip, and as he went he must give warning of his polluted presence with the cry, 'Unclean, unclean!' We see the same thing in the Middle Ages, which merely applied the Mosaic law. The priest, wearing his stole and carrying a crucifix, led the leper into the church, and read the burial service over him. The leper was a man who was already dead, though still alive. He had to wear a black garment that all might recognize and live in a leper-or lazar-house. He must not come into a church service but while the service went on he might peer through the leper 'squint' cut in the walls. The leper had not only to bear the physical pain of his disease; he had to bear the mental anguish and the heart-break of being completely banished from human society and totally shunned." [4]

This woman would have been considered a threat to others: "Uncleanness or impurity is basically defined as that which is a threat to or opposes holiness, and hence must be kept separate from that sphere." [5]

4 Major Contributors and Editors. (2016). J. D. Barry, D. Bomar, D. R. Brown, R. Klippenstein, D. Mangum, C. Sinclair Wolcott, … W. Widder (Eds.), The Lexham Bible Dictionary. Bellingham, WA: Lexham Press.

5 Freedman, D. N. (Ed.). (1992). Unclean and Clean. In The Anchor Yale Bible Dictionary (Vol. 6, p. 729). New York: Doubleday.

After bleeding for twelve long years and being considered unclean, how do you think it would have affected this woman…

Physically	Financially	Relationally	Emotionally	Spiritually

This woman's suffering would have affected all aspects of her life. Physically, she was tired, weak, and hurting from chronic pain. She had been experimented on by a jillion doctors but had gone untouched by loved ones for over a decade; no hugs, no high fives, no kisses, no 'atta girl pats on the back. Financially, she was broke. Emotionally, this woman had to have felt defeated, stuck, lonely, and hopeless. Relationally, she was completely pushed out of community. Someone once said, "Hell is total isolation." This woman lived in total isolation from friends, family, work, school, community, and church. She couldn't go listen to her favorite band jam out. She couldn't play on her rec soccer team. She couldn't date unless she found a hottie with a sicktastic rash who was also considered unclean. She couldn't go to the movie theater or the farmers market without yelling, "Cooties!" warning others about her presence. And she couldn't go to the meeting place of God. She was totally ousted physically, socially, and relationally. This woman spent all she had and instead of getting better, the Bible says, "she grew worse."

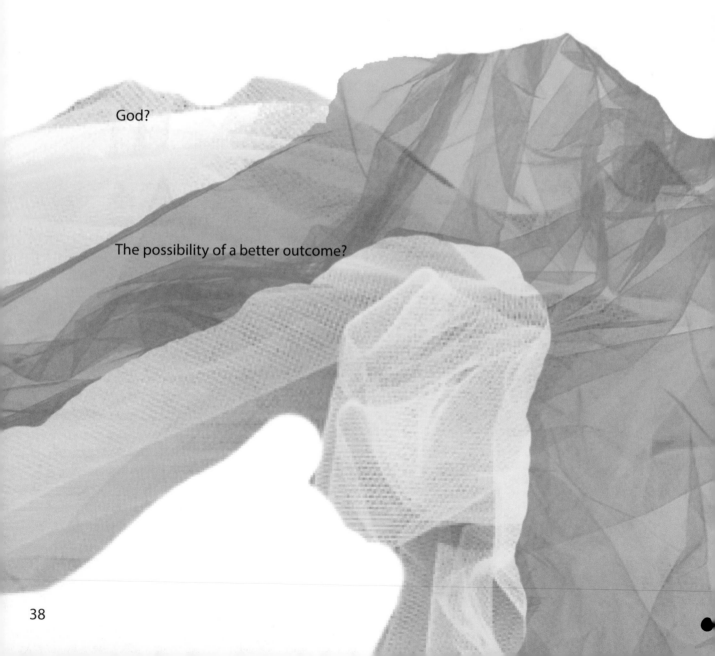

Reflect

What would this experience begin to tell you about

Yourself?

God?

The possibility of a better outcome?

Her circumstance could have easily told her that God is

impersonal and weak.

God is so busy taking care of women being sex trafficked, foster children, hungry kids in Africa, and the lady with breast cancer down the street, so why would He stop and take care of her? Her circumstance could have easily told her that God obviously lacks power, might, ability and capability because He clearly can't seem to bring about the change she needs. She could have thought that God is too big, too mighty, to "other than" to help, or that God is a weanie and has no power to do anything to rescue her from pain and suffering. She could have believed about God what we often do:

- God is detached
- God is indifferent
- God is remote
- God is busy
- God is disinterested
- God is dispassionate
- God is impartial
- God is neglectful
- God doesn't exist

Reflect

What do your difficult circumstances often tell you about who God is?

On a scale of 1 to 10, where do your current circumstances honestly rate God right now?

impersonal	1	2	3	5	6	7	8	9	10	personal
weak	1	2	3	5	6	7	8	9	10	powerful

Circle which one of the following beliefs you most often operate out of. Don't just circle the right answer, actually circle the one you act upon:

God is impersonal and powerful.

God is impersonal and weak.

God is personal and weak.

God is personal and powerful.

How do those beliefs about God inform your hope in what He can do in the midst of your longing?

What do you long for right now and do you believe God is personal and powerful enough to meet you in that longing?

How are you acting upon that belief with your…

attitude?

trust?

hope?

actions?

Ruminate

God is personal

You have searched me, Lord, and you know me. **Psalm 139:1**

My sheep listen to my voice; I know them, and they follow me. **John 10:27**

Jesus replied, "Anyone who loves me will obey my teaching. My Father will love them, and we will come to them and make our home with them." **John 14:23**

I am the vine; you are the branches. If you remain in me and I in you, you will bear much fruit; apart from me you can do nothing. **John 15:5**

Cast all your anxiety on him because he cares for you. **1 Peter 5:7**

See what great love the Father has lavished on us, that we should be called children of God! **1 John 3:1a**

God is powerful

Your right hand, Lord, was majestic in power. Your right hand, Lord, shattered the enemy. **Exodus 15:6**

[29]He gives strength to the weary and increases the power of the weak. [30]Even youths grow tired and weary, and young men stumble and fall; [31]but those who hope in the Lord will renew their strength.They will soar on wings like eagles; they will run and not grow weary, they will walk and not be faint. **Isaiah 40:29-31**

Ah, Sovereign Lord, you have made the heavens and the earth by your great power and outstretched arm. Nothing is too hard for you. **Jeremiah 32:17**

The Lord your God is with you, the Mighty Warrior who saves. He will take great delight in you; in his love he will no longer rebuke you, but will rejoice over you with singing. **Zephaniah 3:17**

Jesus looked at them and said, "With man this is impossible, but with God all things are possible." **Matthew 19:26**

Now to him who is able to do immeasurably more than all we ask or imagine, according to his power that is at work within us. **Ephesians 3:20**

By his power God raised the Lord from the dead, and he will raise us also. **1 Corinthians 6:14**

But he said to me, "My grace is sufficient for you, for my power is made perfect in weakness." Therefore I will boast all the more gladly about my weaknesses, so that Christ's power may rest on me. **2 Corinthians 12:9**

So often we allow our circumstances to tell us who God is and we need to be women who, right smack dab in the midst of isolation, sickness, anxiety attacks, break ups and parenting challenges, tell our circumstances who God is. We need to be women who say, "You know what, hemorrhage? You're the worst but my God is mighty to save. You know what, rejection? You obviously can't see what's right in front of you: God cares about me. You know what, failure? You're a terrible liar but God knows my truth. You know what, death? You act like you have the final say, but God has a way out."

Reflect and Respond

After reading the previous Scriptures, go back and circle the ones you needed to hear most. After you have done that, ask yourself this question: What do I need to claim about God to my circumstances? Write a prayer below doing just that...

God you are... enough for my want.

God you are...

God you are...

...and I'm banking on it, claiming it, trusting it, acting upon it and hoping for it. Lord, be personal and powerful in all the ways you know I need you to be. Amen.

Counselor's Couch

Carrie Cochran

One of Collide's core values is to recognize brokenness so it can be made whole. We have a growing community of women walking toward healing, as well as a community of counselors who are partnering with us to this end. We hope you not only enjoy hearing a counselor's voice here, but that you open yourself up to the transformational work God is calling you into so that you can see His healing as a reality in your life.

Too often the problems we face start to make us feel powerless in our own lives. Sometimes, we begin to accept these problems into our lives, almost without noticing how much power they have taken from us. When I notice I'm feeling overwhelmed by something, I've found it helpful to step back and really take a look at a problem: look over it, around it, and under it, considering factors that missed my attention before. In taking the time to consider the problem doesn't own or control us in all the ways we thought it did, hope can begin to spill back into our vision and we realize we don't feel helpless anymore. There is a process I've found helpful for people who are struggling under the weight of a problem. It can be powerful to be able to see this process all at once when you are finished. Here are the steps:*

1.   **At the top of your paper, name that problem.** For this exercise, the best problem to define is one that you have some control over. So instead of naming a person from a difficult relationship, name the consequence of the relationship on you (insecurity, fear, inferiority, being a doormat or caretaker, etc.). You can do this exercise naming a medical issue, but it also works to dig a little deeper underneath and name what the diagnosis or injury has brought up in you (fear of the future, forgotten by God, fatigue, anger towards/on behalf of someone).

2.   A metaphor can help you look at the problem from an emotional or sensory viewpoint. For example, the problem might feel like an avalanche, a trapdoor, freezing wind, tornado, quicksand, a tidal wave, an earthquake, a dark cloud. All of these pictures have slightly different feelings associated, so your metaphor is personal to how you feel when

* Example on page 48

the problem attempts to take over. Your metaphor may also give you some clues as to how the problem has tricked you into giving it power (maybe it comes on suddenly, or maybe it sneaks up on you slowly, or maybe it comes disguised as a coping method). **Write your metaphor (or draw it) near the name of your problem.**

3. **On the left side of your paper, list what this problem brings with it.** When that wind or cloud comes blowing in, what changes do you notice in yourself?

4. **On the right side, list what you could be doing if the problem stopped coming into your life.** What can you imagine having the time, energy, or joy for if you weren't worrying about the problem?

5. As you consider your first two lists (the combined cost of the problem to your life), **in the middle of your paper, list your feelings towards the problem.** This is your chance to be totally real with yourself.

6. Take a moment to evaluate whether your problem meets any needs. Some problems clearly don't help in any way, and you can skip this step and #7. However, some problems actually started out as ways to cope with something else but became big problems all on their own (sometimes much worse than the original problem you were trying to cope with). Some examples of coping problems might be drinking to ease social anxiety, shopping to block out relationship stress, gaming for depression, eating issues for anxiety, or social media to numb work stress. For coping problems, sometimes we aren't actually aware of why we started it in the first place, and then before we know it, the new problem generalizes into other areas of life. **On the lower-left-middle section of your paper, for a problem like this, list any need the problem may still be meeting.**

7. **On the lower-right-middle section, list ways other than the problem to get the needs met listed in step #5.** This is your chance to be open and really brainstorm what other ways of coping might work better for you, no matter how unrealistic they might seem right now.

As you look over the **problem map**, you can now make some connections about how this problem is truly impacting your life. You may also see the beginning of a plan to change things up. You may see some hope that you just might have some other options.

If you find that you have new insight and ideas, but still feel pretty powerless to fight this problem, then consider adding some support in your life. Counseling, a general recovery group, a specific support group targeting this problem, a close friend, mentor, or sponsor are all great options for enlisting help in taking the power back from the problem. As Christ-followers, we also have the support of the One who created us and knows all things, including every problem we will ever face. When we lose our way, He lights the way back home. It is my hope that the problem on your map has already lost some of its power in your life. You may just find that your new clarity brings courage and hope, a powerful duo.

I keep my eyes always on the Lord. With him at my right hand, I will not be shaken. **Psalm 16:8**

The spirit and ideas for this exercise are respectfully adapted from Playful Approaches to Serious Problems: Narrative Therapy with Children and Their Families by Jennifer Freeman, David Epston, and Dean Lobovits.

Fear of the Future

Anxiety
Sadness
Questions
Disappointment

Enjoying the
present
Making plans
Looking for
opportunities

Anger
Resentment
Sorrow

Need to feel wanted
Need to feel important
Need to feel needed

Other relationships
Work
Ministry
Volunteer Work

Risk Hoping Again 4

personal &
powerful

Read

²⁵And a woman was there who had been subject to bleeding for twelve years. ²⁶She had suffered a great deal under the care of many doctors and had spent all she had, yet instead of getting better she grew worse. ²⁷When she heard about Jesus, she came up behind him in the crowd and touched his cloak, ²⁸because she thought, "If I just touch his clothes, I will be healed."
Mark 5:25-28

As you can imagine, this woman could have easily thought, "God couldn't care less if I just rot here and die. God has abandoned me. God doesn't see my life and dreams as worthy to save. God plays favorites and I'm not one. God thinks I need to learn another lesson. God is powerless to help." And like us, if these things be true, to hope in God for a different outcome will only set us up for more disappointment.

I mean, how many times can you keep trying for the baby? And how many times can you show up as the third wheel, hoping to be the first choice? And how many times can you pray for the cancer to go away and it keeps coming back? And how many times can you hope they quit drinking but they never do? This woman could've said, "I've prayed a million prayers, followed all the doctors orders, and woken up for twelve long years hoping it was just a dream, but this nightmare continues to be my reality." When the story doesn't go the way we want it to, it's so easy to give up on hope.

Reflect

Have you ever felt let down by hope? If so, in what way(s)?

How does hope make you feel vulnerable with God?

How does hope sometimes feel like it sets you up for more disappointment?

I recently worked on a ministry project with a woman whose dream of being an actress had been dashed. She had worked so hard towards this goal and had experienced opportunities and promises that seemed like they were going to work out, only to have them fall through. After experiencing hope, over and over again she kept experiencing rejection. She and her husband had to move to the Pacific Northwest, away from the land of Hollywood and the many job opportunities she had dreamed of. She was trying to find God in the midst of losing her identity and ideas of who she always thought she'd be. Then she got pregnant. So much hope came with this new life and new season.

She lost the baby.

This woman who has been full of faith her entire life has begun to give up as she has faced loss after loss. It's not that she's despondent or depressed. It's more that she doesn't feel like she has the emotional capacity to continue hoping and being let down. And yet it's in this place of no longer wanting to hold out hope, that she feels stuck, lifeless, distant from God and unexcited about her future. Her decision to no longer hope that a better outcome is possible is almost as painful as the circumstances that led her there.

Reflect

Like the aspiring actress facing rejection and miscarriage, how do you see women around you struggling to want to hope again?

How could the bleeding woman in **Mark 5** have given up on hope?

Why is it so difficult to hope for a different outcome than the one that keeps you stuck?

Believing a different outcome is possible, can feel...

disappointing
foolish
hopeful

Ruminate

The woman in **Mark 5** could have felt all those things you listed on the previous page, but hope was all she realized she had. Ruminate on the following Scriptures:

You will be secure, because there is hope; you will look about you and take your rest in safety. **Job 11:18**

Yes, my soul, find rest in God; my hope comes from him. **Psalm 62:5**

You wearied yourself by such going about, but you would not say, 'It is hopeless.' You found renewal of your strength, and so you did not faint. **Isaiah 57:10**

And hope does not put us to shame, because God's love has been poured out into our hearts through the Holy Spirit, who has been given to us. **Romans 5:5**

For in this hope we were saved. But hope that is seen is no hope at all. Who hopes for what they already have? **Romans 8:24**

He has delivered us from such a deadly peril, and he will deliver us again. On him we have set our hope that he will continue to deliver us. **2 Corinthians 1:10**

Command those who are rich in this present world not to be arrogant nor to put their hope in wealth, which is so uncertain, but to put their hope in God, who richly provides us with everything for our enjoyment. **1 Timothy 6:17**

We want each of you to show this same diligence to the very end, so that what you hope for may be fully realized. **Hebrews 6:11**

According to each of the Scriptures on the previous page, what does hope do?

In what area of your life have you given up hoping for a different outcome than the one you already have?

Hope is always a risk. You're absolutely right. Hope always risks your faith looking like a fool. It risks your vulnerability exposing you. It risks your dreams looking silly. It risks your disappointment going viral. But not hoping risks too. You risk your heart closing up. You risk getting bitter and cynical. You risk making God too small and your problems too big. You risk no longer working or walking towards the life you hope to see.

The bleeding woman could have easily second guessed reaching out for help because if she touched Jesus, she risked causing a riot. She would make Him and everyone else surrounding her "unclean." That risk had the potential to make her feel even more alone. She had to have thought, "Why bother? God hasn't helped me yet? Why would He today? And besides, He's busy doing important things like healing sick kids." For whatever reason, she did what was least expected: she fought the crowd to get what she wanted. She moved toward Jesus, reached out and participated in her own healing.

Reflect

What strikes you about her risk?

How can you take a cue from this woman's hope?

Risk hoping again and when you find yourself saying, "again?" yes, again. Hope is all you have. Hope is what leads the way when you have no way. Hope is what keeps your heart tender when it risks getting callused. Hope is what stretches your reach and feeds your faith. Hope is what keeps your dreams alive because if they die, they stand no chance to ever live. Hope is what finds you touching the hem of the only One who has the power to touch your disappointment and bring it the healing it needs. It's time to show back up to hope.

Risk hoping again, friend.

Respond

Spend time today journaling here, asking God to help you risk hoping again…

Counselor's Couch

Shawn Hofing

One of Collide's core values is to recognize brokenness so it can be made whole. We have a growing community of women walking toward healing, as well as a community of counselors who are partnering with us to this end. We hope you not only enjoy hearing a counselor's voice here, but that you open yourself up to the transformational work God is calling you into so that you can see His healing as a reality in your life.

I have a growing and firm conviction that the questions we ask ourselves and others are vitally important. The reason for this is aptly stated in the poetry of E.E. Cummings. He wrote, "Always the beautiful answer who asks a more beautiful question." Jesus Himself was notoriously and masterfully good at asking people beautiful questions. Sometimes He would even answer people's question, with another question, inviting them to ask a better question that will help lead them to a deeper revelation of the story of God, who is love, and their place in it.

In my work as a therapist, I listen to people's beautiful questions, and when they are feeling stuck, I try to help them find and ask a more beautiful question, to help get them unstuck. For example, a common question many people ask, either implicitly or explicitly, when they enter my office is, "Why should I hope again when it hasn't worked before?" In my experience, questions that begin with "why" aren't usually very helpful or generative when first starting out. The reason for this is because our brains function a lot like Google's search engine bar. As soon as we enter a question, our top five most recent and/or frequent searches will appear with the answer. The problem is that for most of us, those most recent answers are usually covered in shame and/or blame, telling us that we shouldn't hope again because we aren't worth it, and/or that nobody cares. Such answers are not helpful, or generative, and only serve to leave us stuck in a cycle of cynicism, despair, and hopelessness.

One of the best ways to break the cycle is to start with a more beautiful question. I have found that when first starting out, the more helpful and generative questions usually begin with a "what" or a "how." For instance, instead of asking, "Why should I hope again when it hasn't worked before?" it is often more helpful to ask, "How can I hope again when it hasn't worked before?" The new question invites the Google search engine part of our brains, both on a conscious and unconscious level, to start looking for new more generative answers. Here is an example of what I mean. On the one hand the question could be heard as a cry of pain and despair, thus inviting an answer from the Google search engine part of our brain that encourages us to tell our story, name our pain, and learn how to grieve and lament. On the other hand the question could be heard as a request for advice, thus inviting an answer from the Google search engine part of our brain that encourages us to seek out practical tools that will help to expand our imagination and learn a new way forward. Either way, it is evident that re-framing the question invites responses that are more likely to lead us to a place of healing and growth, rather than shame and despair.

Learning the art and skill of asking beautiful questions takes practice. It is also a skill that is best learned within the context of relationships and community. This is because it is often through relationships that we not only learn new questions but also, like Jesus, question the questions in kindness and love. May you find a place to ask your beautiful questions, and may those beautiful questions lead you to a deeper revelation of the story of God, who is love, and your place in it.

If  5

personal &
powerful

Read

²⁷ When she heard about Jesus, she came up behind him in the crowd and touched his cloak, ²⁸ because she thought, "If I just touch his clothes, I will be healed." **Mark 5:27-28**

Apparently it was taught in that day and age that there were eleven ways to cure her kind of sickness. The things she was encouraged to try were weird like "carrying the ashes of an ostrich egg in a linen rag in summer and a cotton rag in winter."[6] My guess is, she tried every one of those "cures" because that's what we do when we get desperate for change. We can often think "if I just" get a man, go to a naturopath, lose 20 pounds, snarf on spinach, apply essential oils to my ear lobes, and pray using bigger words, I will get the life I want. We will try everything before we try Jesus. We will even try the keto diet before we try God.

Reflect

What are some of the "if I justs" you have been encouraged to try to make your life better?

> If I just...

6 Barclay, W. (2001). The New Daily Study Bible: The Gospel of Mark (p. 148). Edinburgh: Saint Andrew Press.

The Bible says all of the bleeding woman's "if i justs" left her worse off than when she first began. Can you think of ways you have seen in your own life, and those around you, how our "if I justs" make us worse off?

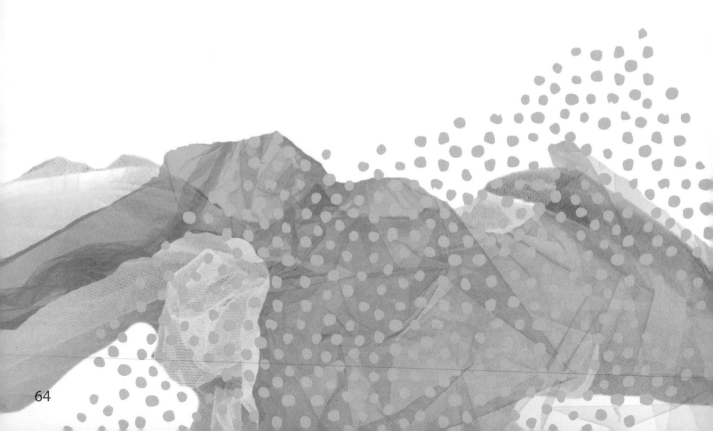

Fill in the missing parts of the table.

Person	Scripture	Their "if I just"	How it left them d off
Rebekah	Genesis 27:5–10 Genesis 27:42–45	If I just trick my husband	She had to send her son away
	Genesis 30:1–5	If I just have kids	She pushed her husband to sleep with another woman
	Luke 10:38–42		
	John 4:4–26		She was more thirsty and seeking to quench that thirst
Judas	Matthew 26:14–16 Matthew 27:1–5		
	Luke 22:54–62	If I just deny my alliance to Jesus	
Ananias and Sapphira	Acts 5:1–10	If I just make myself look good	
You			

As you can see, our "if I justs" often land us in a worse place than we started. And the same was true for this woman who had been hemorrhaging. She had tried a jillion things and none of them worked, except for this one "if I just…"

65

Reflect

What does it take to reach out for help when very little has helped?

Why do you think God is often our last "if I just…?"

What do you see as the significance of the moment when the woman came up behind Jesus and touched His cloak?

Is our reach for God only worth it if the story goes exactly how we want it to when we touch Him?

Ruminate

In the book of Daniel in the Old Testament, when three exiles in Babylon rebelled against a decree to worship an image of gold made by King Nebuchadnezzar, the king ordered them to be thrown into a blazing furnace and asked, *"What god will be able to rescue you from my hand?"* **Daniel 3:15**

Daniel 3:16-18 describes how they respond:
*[16]Shadrach, Meshach and Abednego replied to him, "King Nebuchadnezzar, we do not need to defend ourselves before you in this matter. [17]If we are thrown into the blazing furnace, the God we serve is able to deliver us from it, and he will deliver us from Your Majesty's hand. [18]But **<u>even if</u>** he does not, we want you to know, Your Majesty, that we will not serve your gods or worship the image of gold you have set up."*

What strikes you about Shadrach, Meshach and Abednego's "even if" response to the king?

Nevertheless!

Martin Luther King, Jr. delivered one of his most fiery and amazing sermons based on this passage in Daniel, in a Baptist church in 1967. He titled his sermon "But If Not." He said regarding this passage, "This simply means, my friends, that the ultimate test of one's faith is his ability to say, 'But if not.' You see there is what you may call an 'if' faith, and there is a 'though' faith. And the permanent faith, the lasting, the powerful faith is the 'though' faith. Now the 'if' faith says, 'If all goes well; if life is hopeful, prosperous and happy; if I don't have to go to jail; if I don't have to face the agonies and burdens of life; if I'm not ever called bad names because of taking a stand that I feel that I must take; if none of these things happen, then I'll have faith in God, then I'll be alright.' That's the 'if' faith. You know, a lot of people have the 'if' faith… There is a 'though' faith, though. And the 'though' faith says, 'Though things go wrong; though evil is temporarily triumphant; though sickness comes and the cross looms, nevertheless! I'm gonna believe anyway and I'm gonna have faith anyway; though the waters thereof roar and be troubled, though the mountains shake with the swelling thereof, the LORD of hosts is with us; the God of Jacob is our refuge."[7]

Reflect

Martin Luther King, Jr. challenges us to think about what kind of faith we have. Do you have an "if" faith or a "though" faith?

7 https://www.youtube.com/watch?v=pOjpalO2seY

How much does your faith rely on your circumstances?

How much does your faith rely on you getting what you ask for when you reach out to God?

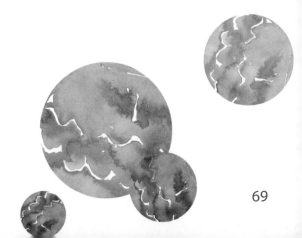

Think about where you are at right now… can you say, "though I am going through hardship, turmoil and struggle, my God is with me?" Take some time to recognize the place you're in ("though I am") and allow yourself to claim who God is despite that hard place ("God is").

Though...	God is...
I am struggling to find what I'm "made to do"	all-knowing and has a plan
my enemies are telling people convincing stories about me	my defender
I'm standing up for what is right and it's causing issues	a God who promises to bless the righteous

"The fiery furnace

couldn't stop them

from believing"

Martin Luther King Jr.

What if this bleeding woman had reached out to God every one of the last 11 years and 364 days to no avail? If you were her, would you have reached out one more time even though you hadn't gotten what you wanted the last 4,379 days?

Martin Luther King, Jr. closes up his sermon with this: "…I say to you this morning, if you have never found something so dear and so precious to you that you will die for it, then you aren't fit to live. You may be 38 years old as I happen to be. One day some great opportunity stands before you and calls upon you to stand up for some great principle, some great issue, some great cause--you refuse to do it because you are afraid; you refuse to do it because you want to live longer; you're afraid that you will lose your job, or you're afraid that you will be criticized or that you will lose your popularity or you're afraid that somebody will stab you or shoot at you or bomb your house. So you refuse to take the stand. Well you may go on and live until you are 90, but you're just as dead at 38 as you would be at 90! And the cessation of breathing in your life is but the belated announcement of an earlier death of the spirit. You died when you refused to stand up for right, you died when you refused to stand up for truth, you died when you refused to stand up for justice. These boys stand before us today, and I thank God for them, for they had found something. The fiery furnace couldn't stop them from believing. They said, 'Throw us into the fiery furnace.' But you

Transformed

"Somehow that burning fiery furnace was transformed into an air-conditioned living room." Martin Luther King Jr.

know the interesting thing is, the Bible talks about a miracle. Because they had faith enough to say 'But if not,' God was with them as an eternal companion. And this is what I want to say finally, that there is a reward if you do right for righteousness' sake. It says that somehow that burning fiery furnace was transformed into an air-conditioned living room. Somebody looked in there and said, 'We put three in here, but now we see four.' Don't ever think you're by yourself. Go on to jail if necessary but you'll never go alone. Take a stand for that which is right, and the world may misunderstand you and criticize you, but you never go alone, for somewhere I read that, one with God is a majority, and God has a way of transforming a minority into a majority... tell the world that you're going with truth. You're going with justice, you're going with goodness, and you will have an eternal companionship. And the world will look at you and they won't understand you, for your fiery furnace will be around you, but you'll go on anyhow. But if not, I will not bow, and God grant that we will never bow before the gods of evil."[8] (To listen to this powerful sermon in its entirety, search YouTube for "Martin Luther King Jr. But If Not")

8 https://www.youtube.com/watch?v=pOjpalO2seY

Many would look at Martin Luther King, Jr.'s life and say that it was his faith that was willing to walk into the fiery furnace trusting God "even if" that made it possible for his life to rally a needed and unprecedented movement that changed history and worked toward fighting racism and oppression. His fight for justice had ripple effects on the entire world, and still does over 50 years after his death.

In the midst of hardship, evil, suffering, an overwhelming fight that feels like you're losing, and a fiery furnace you might get tossed into, you can be a woman whose first and only "If I just" is always reaching out to Jesus believing day in and day out that "even if" the story doesn't go the way you want it to,

"My God, He is with me. He is with me so I can reach for Him, travel to Him, touch His hem and beg of Him.

He will always be found by me and me by Him."

"But if not, I *will not* bow." - Martin Luther King, Jr.

Respond

Take some time to talk to God today. Feel free to write a prayer using this prompt or have a conversation with Him...

God,
Even if...

Amen.

A Transaction 6

personal & powerful

Read

²⁹Immediately her bleeding stopped and she felt in her body that she was freed from her suffering. ³⁰At once Jesus realized that power had gone out from him. **Mark 5:29-30a**

The Bible says the moment she reached out to touch Jesus, her bleeding immediately stopped and she was freed from her suffering. At once, Jesus realized power had gone out from Him, onto her. A transaction of sorts took place. I don't think we often realize this, but Jesus knew that every collision that brought someone life, would bring Him death. He knew there would be a painful exchange on the cross.

Isaiah 53 talks about this transaction... *"By His wounds we are healed."* We see that Jesus would wear every garment soaked with shame. He would be mocked for every abusive word they ever uttered. He would be stoned so the woman caught in the act of adultery wouldn't be. He would be blinded by darkness, unable to see, so others could walk in the light. He would suffer the pain that caused every tear. He would bleed so this woman could be freed. If there ever was someone who could say, "Me too. I feel your pain," it's Jesus. When power went out from Jesus to heal this woman, trust me, it was skin off His back.

Reflect

What does this passage indicate happened to heal the woman?

 What strikes you about the idea that when power left Jesus and stopped her bleeding, it would cause His bleeding on the cross?

Ruminate

Let's process the idea that with every collision where Jesus ran into a wounded person and healed them, He would end up taking on their wound. Use the blank spaces to come up with your own examples.

Person Jesus collided with who received healing	Scripture passage	The wound Jesus would take on
Man born blind	**John 9:1-7**	*Surrounded by darkness*
Adulteress	**John 8:1-11**	*Condemnation*
Woman bent over by a spirit	**Luke 13:10-17**	
	John 4:5-41	*Thirst*
	Matthew 9:32-33	

How does the exercise on the previous page change your view of the cross when you think of so many of Jesus' collisions with wounded people?

How do you feel when you consider the ways God has brought you healing, knowing He freely took your wounds upon Himself?

⁴Surely he took up our pain

and bore our suffering,

yet we considered him punished by God,

stricken by him, and afflicted.

⁵But he was pierced for our transgressions,

he was crushed for our iniquities;

the punishment that brought us peace was on him,

and by his wounds we are healed.

⁶We all, like sheep, have gone astray,

each of us has turned to our own way;

and the Lord has laid on him

the iniquity of us all.

⁷He was oppressed and afflicted,

yet he did not open his mouth;

he was led like a lamb to the slaughter,

and as a sheep before its shearers is silent,

so he did not open his mouth.

Isaiah 53: 4-7

Go back through the Isaiah passage on the previous page, and circle all the places you find the words "our" and "us".

Write everything this passage says Jesus took on that was ours.

Circle below which of the following words out of Jesus' experience you can resonate with.

pain	astray
suffering	iniquity
punishment	oppression
stricken	led to slaughter
affliction	silent

What strikes you about the idea that we have a God who looks at our pain and says, "Me too?"

What strikes you about the idea that we can look at God's pain and say, "Me too," to Him as well?

You can say, "me too," to Jesus and He can say, "me too," to you.

Reflect

The Bible says the bleeding woman was "freed from her suffering"- what do you think that must have felt like?

Every Time you read about a collision with Jesus where a healing took place, whether it be in the New Testament, or in your neighbor, your kid or your own life, there was an ultimate wounded collision that took place on the cross... one where Jesus took upon Himself all of our pain and suffering so that we might go free.

Read about the Ultimate Wounded Collision in **Matthew 27:27-50.**

Reflect

When you know that this woman's healing came at Jesus' expense, how does that change this story in **Mark 5** for you?

What does the cross tell you about Jesus' love, that is willing to transact your healing in exchange for His pain?

Respond

Knowing that it's God's desire to free His girls, including you, even if it means He bleeds, how do you want to respond? There's nothing that God won't do for you. There's no road He won't travel. There's no mountain He won't climb. There's no rock that will go unturned. There's no assignment He won't take. There's no mess He won't enter. There's no pain or mistake He won't wear. Take some time today to come before God in gratitude for His desire to free you.

Look at the Stars

personal & powerful

Read

He turned around in the crowd and asked, "Who touched my clothes?" [31] "You see the people crowding against you," his disciples answered, "and yet you can ask, 'Who touched me?' " [32] But Jesus kept looking around to see who had done it. **Mark 5:30b-32**

Imagine This Scene… a lot of people might have bumped into Jesus, stepped on His feet, or shook His hand. He was in a crowd after all and that's what happens when we're in crowds. We rub shoulders with people, we get pushed, shoved, impatient, sweaty and for those of us who have space bubbles, they get violated. In a crowd, power went out from Jesus onto this woman and there seemed to be something significant to Him about their interaction. It was so significant to Him, that it made Him stop.

Reflect

Even the disciples wondered why Jesus was asking this question. Why do you think He cared to know who touched Him?

Why do you think Jesus didn't just move on and keep walking toward healing the dying girl?

Jesus had places to go and people to heal and plenty of power where that came from. JR Edwards says, "Jesus is not content to dispatch a miracle; he wants to encounter a person."[9] You know, I wonder, do we merely want God's miracles but not God Himself? This might be enough for us but it's not enough for Him. This woman wanted relief, but Jesus wanted relationship.

9 Edwards, J. R. (2002). The Gospel according to Mark (p. 165). Grand Rapids, MI; Leicester, England: Eerdmans; Apollos.

Reflect

How does it strike you that Jesus is not just content to dispatch a miracle, but He wants to encounter you?

If you were to evaluate your "conversations" with God (your prayers, your requests, your praises, your laments), do you spend most of your time seeking Him for what He can do for you, or seeking Him for who He is?

Do you merely want God's miracles or God Himself?

Why do you think miracles without relationship are often enough for us?

Think about an important relationship other than the one you have with God... would it be enough for that person to only "do things" for you, but not to engage in relationship with you?

Why do you put God in a relational box you would never consider putting others in, where it has often become okay for you to merely want what God can do for you more than you want God Himself?

We have a God who is so personal, Scripture says He knows our name. He knows the number of hairs on our head. He keeps track of all our sorrows, keeping our tears in a bottle, recording each one in His journal. God knows the day you will be born before you're born and He knows the day you will move from this temporary place to your forever home. God knows your maiden name, your married name and the names you call yourself. God knows your birthmark because He stamped you and He knows the untapped gifts you're afraid to use. He knows the way you snort when you laugh and why you burst out crying in your car all alone. He knows you're allergic to pineapple and that's why He made strawberries. God knows your going out and your lying down. God doesn't need a "Find Your Friends" app to locate you. He knows where you are and He knows how you're doing. You're so busy lately, you don't even know how you are doing, but God knows.

Ruminate

Look up the Scriptures below and describe the ways God personally knows each one of us.

Verse	God is personal
Isaiah 43:1	God calls me by name
Psalm 56:8	
Psalm 139:1-6	
Psalm 139:16	
Luke 12:7	

Long before I called you, I saw you.

Jesus showed His omniscience when He helped the woman at the well see her pattern with men before she even shared it. He showed this ability when He called out Judas' betrayal before the betrayal. He showed His foreknowledge over and over again warning His disciples: I'm gonna die. You watch, but don't worry, three days later, I'm gonna show you Who has all the power. And He showed His all-knowingness with Nathaniel, whose mind was so blown that he asked, *"How do you know me?"* **John 1:48a**. Jesus responded with this sense… Long before I called you, I saw you.

Reflect

Do you look for God with expectancy, or do you tend to assume He's doing His own thing and you're doing yours?

Do you expect God to meet you in personal ways or do you kind of think He already did His job... made the Earth, gave life and now the rest is on you?

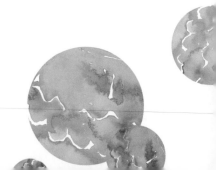

How does the idea of God turning around in response to your reach because He personally wants to encounter you, challenge the ideas you have about God being distant, busy, and impersonal?

When I started to wonder about the idea of a Creator, a Supernatural, Bigger-than-me Being, who might have arranged and ordered things just so, my biggest hang up was answering the question, "Where was this God when I needed Him as a kid?" I certainly wasn't considering Jesus, but just the idea of a God who placed the stars in the sky and made you and me… I was looking into that.

The more I looked, the more I began to see.

I remember as a little five year old girl getting kicked out of my house by an angry drunk man in the middle of the night. Maybe I was defiant, maybe I talked back. All I know is that I refused to wake up at 1 a.m. and do what was being asked. My refusal met his insistence. I remember having this suitcase that I had been waiting to use for my first visit to this dad I heard I had and could see one day soon. I shoved as many of my clothes I could fit in it and walked out onto Main Street. I will never forget walking in the snow with my white suitcase, having no idea where I was going. I had this moment where I scanned my little kid mental file of people I could turn to for help and an inner panic set in that told me I was walking away from the one person in that file. I remember thinking, "I could really use a dad right about now."

The more you look, the more you'll begin to see.

91

We are all in the gutter, but some of us are looking at the stars - Oscar Wilde,

Everything was still. I looked up at the expanse of the sky. Snowflakes fell on my face. The open road ahead of me was lit up by the moon. The sky in my hometown might be the most beautiful vault of heaven you'll ever see. I mean, I know we share the same sky, you and I, but the Roslyn sky, full of stars, surrounded by evergreen trees, it's almost like they embrace you in moments where all you need is to be held.

Oscar Wilde said, "We are all in the gutter, but some of us are looking at the stars."[10]

Sometimes, looking up is all we can do, when we're 5 and when we're 55.

A quote often attributed to Martin Luther says,

"God writes the Gospel not in the Bible alone, but also on trees, and in the flowers and clouds and stars."

The only gospel or good news I had in that moment was in the constellations above, the ridge that hemmed me in, and the moon that told me despite how I felt in it's light, I was not alone. Every step down that road got me closer to wanting to be wanted and needing my Father to come.

10 Wilde, Oscar. Lady Windermere's Fan.

Fifteen years later, as a 21-year-old college student, I handed my hurting, broken life to Jesus Christ saying, "I can't do this on my own." Within a week of my unlikely conversion I stepped foot into a church, and days after that a woman showed up at my work and in a British voice said, "I knew you when you were a little girl and I need to talk to you." This woman was in charge of the communication cards, which I filled out at the church I had randomly walked into. She said, "I used to watch you play on the streets of Roslyn and God told me you would go through pain and you would need Him. I prayed for you for all these years and here, 15 years later, across the state, you walked into my church and handed your life to Christ."

I had felt alone most my life, but I now see that

I have been surrounded.

I think Jesus asked, "Who touched me?" because He wanted the bleeding woman to know that He sees her and always has. I think He wants you to know that too. He sees you, friend.

> He sees your dimple.
> He sees your Visa bill.
> He sees your insecurity in that room.
> He sees your ugly arguments with your partner.
> He sees how you tear up at the thought of using your gifts and passions.
> He sees your unmatched socks and your "dirty laundry."
> He sees your procrastination.
> He sees the way you numb your pain.
> He sees what's bleeding even if you have become accustomed to it.
> He sees your longing, your heart's desire, and your unmet dreams.

God sees you. And all He's ever wanted is for you to know not only does He see you, but He's coming for you. He's moving mountains for you. He's on a passionate pursuit to find you because you've wandered away and gotten a little lost. He's been there and He's not going anywhere. You can run from Him, you can hide, you can act like He's not there. You can even blame Him. But He's walking with you down all the roads you'll ever find yourself walking. He's there… as much as the stars in the sky and the trees on the ridge. He's hemmed you in with His presence and He's committed to being found by you and you by Him.

Reflect

How do you struggle to believe God sees you?

What painful road have you walked down that made you wonder if God is really with you?

How has your pain kept you from allowing yourself to be seen and found by God?

As you look back upon your life, what are some ways you have experienced what only could have been God because it was so uniquely tailored to you, who you are, your needs, your hopes and your longings?

How does hearing other people's stories about God being personal and powerful give you hope for your own story?

Sometimes all we can do is look at the stars. Sometimes we walk hard roads. Sometimes we collide with pain and addiction, abandonment and demands, grouchy neighbors and stinky kimchi. Sometimes we collide with miscarriage and job loss. Sometimes we collide with anger and judgment, cattiness, and religious persecution. And in all these wounded collisions we can easily find ourselves walking some lonely road, wondering if anyone is coming for us. Upon every step, look up at the stars and remember you are surrounded. Even if you can't see it doesn't mean it isn't true. Let the stars remind you that the God who placed them in the sky, the One who made you and me, He walks down every road you walk.

Your father is coming for you.

Respond

How are you waiting for your Father to come for you, even now? Spend some time today reaching out by faith, trusting He's here and His rescue is on the way.

Father, will you come for me on the road I find myself walking...

The Whole Truth

personal &
powerful

Read

30At once Jesus realized that power had gone out from him. He turned around in the crowd and asked, "Who touched my clothes?" 31"You see the people crowding against you," his disciples answered, "and yet you can ask, 'Who touched me?'" 32But Jesus kept looking around to see who had done it. 33Then the woman, knowing what had happened to her, came and fell at his feet and, trembling with fear, told him the whole truth. 34He said to her, "Daughter, your faith has healed you. Go in peace and be freed from your suffering." **Mark 5:30-34**

As soon as Jesus looked around to see who had touched Him, this woman came and fell at His feet and though she was scared as heck to do it, she told Him her whole truth. I love that. I love that her response to God wanting relationship with her was to fully open herself up to be known.

The very fact that she told Him her whole truth, helps us draw a few conclusions. One is that she didn't come to Him with partial truths. I think we do that a lot with each other and with God. We give away parts of ourselves. We let God into some rooms, but not all of them. We tell Him the nice things, the good intentions, the high hopes and the spiritual blah, blah, blah. We allow Him to know about the student debt we need to magically pay off, but we don't let Him know about the leftovers we still have from some of our darkest college experiences. We let God know about our plans for next year but we don't let Him know about the ways we lied at work to advance ourselves for an upcoming promotion. We let God know our worries about our kids, but we don't always let Him know about the ways we project our own childhood pain into creating those worries.

God wants all of us. He doesn't want just part. He doesn't just want your Sunday. He wants your Monday through Saturday too. He doesn't just want your present. He also wants your past. He doesn't just want your hemorrhage. He wants all the ways your bleeding made you bitter. He doesn't just want your "please" and "thank you's." He wants your pleading and your begging, your grief and your rage. God wants all of you. He wants to come into every room in your house, every crevice you've got, every wound that hurts, every dream unmet, and He wants to bring healing and hope. But here's the deal, He can't do any of that if you only give Him parts of you.

This woman gave Him the whole thing. That tells me there was more to her story than a woman we can only assume got a terrible bout of "sickness" and suffered entirely too long. Maybe her whole truth included confession of the nasty places she went with her attitude toward God. Maybe her poured out story told chapters of all the ways she tried to heal herself. Maybe her vulnerable divulgence looked like the hurtful claims others made about her. Maybe the whole truth was uglier, messier, more complicated and more beautiful than we can even begin to imagine. I think this is true because I think it's true for me and I think it's true for you.

So often we don't tell God our whole truth because we don't think He can handle what we've got going on. I want to spend some time challenging your ideas of what God can handle. We are making Him way smaller than He is. We are shrinking His capacity, His patience, His grace, and His forgiveness. God can handle your pain, your sins, your anger, your doubt, your waywardness, and your weaknesses.

Ruminate

How have you been made to believe that God can't handle your **pain**?

Contrary to your belief, God can handle your **pain**:

When (Jesus) saw the crowds, **he had compassion** on them, because they were harassed and helpless, like sheep without a shepherd. **Matthew 9:36**

He **heals the brokenhearted** and binds up their wounds. **Psalm 147:3**

News about him spread all over Syria, and people brought to him all who were ill with various diseases, those suffering severe pain, the demon-possessed, those having seizures, and the paralyzed; and **he healed them**. **Matthew 4:24**

⁴Surely he took up our pain and bore our suffering, yet we considered him punished by God, stricken by him, and afflicted. ⁵But he was pierced for our transgressions, he was crushed for our iniquities; the punishment that brought us peace was on him, and **by his wounds we are healed**. Isaiah 53:4-5

How have you been made to believe that God can't handle your **sin**?

Contrary to your belief, God can handle your **sin**:

*[11]When the Pharisees saw this, they asked his disciples, "Why does your teacher eat with tax collectors and sinners?" [12]On hearing this, Jesus said, "It is not the healthy who need a doctor, but the sick. [13]But go and learn what this means: 'I desire mercy, not sacrifice.' For **I have not come to call the righteous, but sinners."** **Matthew 9:11-13***

*But God demonstrates his own love for us in this: While we were still sinners, **Christ died for us**.* **Romans 5:8**

*"Come now, **let us settle the matter**," says the Lord. "Though your sins are like scarlet, they shall be as white as snow; though they are red as crimson, they shall be like wool.* **Isaiah 1:18**

How have you been made to believe that God can't handle your **anger**?

Contrary to your belief, God can handle your **anger**:

*[32]When Mary reached the place where Jesus was and saw him, she fell at his feet and said, "Lord, if you had been here, my brother would not have died." [33]When Jesus saw her weeping, and the Jews who had come along with her also weeping, he was **deeply moved** in spirit and troubled.* **John 11:32-33**

*[2]How long, Lord, must I call for help, but you do not listen? Or cry out to you, "Violence!" but you do not save? [3]Why do you make me look at injustice? Why do you tolerate wrongdoing? Destruction and violence are before me; there is strife, and conflict bounds. [4]Therefore the law is paralyzed, and justice never prevails. The wicked hem in the righteous, so that justice is perverted. (The Lord's answer) [5]"Look at the nations and watch—and be utterly amazed. For **I am going to do something** in your days that you would not believe, even if you were told.* **Habakkuk 1:2-5**

101

How have you been made to believe that God can't handle your **doubt**?

Contrary to your belief, God can handle your **doubt**:

*[17] A man in the crowd answered, "Teacher, I brought you my son, who is possessed by a spirit that has robbed him of speech. [18] Whenever it seizes him, it throws him to the ground. He foams at the mouth, gnashes his teeth and becomes rigid. I asked your disciples to drive out the spirit, but they could not." [19] "You unbelieving generation," Jesus replied, "how long shall I stay with you? How long shall I put up with you? Bring the boy to me." [20] So they brought him. When the spirit saw Jesus, it immediately threw the boy into a convulsion. He fell to the ground and rolled around, foaming at the mouth. [21] Jesus asked the boy's father, "How long has he been like this?" "From childhood," he answered. [22] "It has often thrown him into fire or water to kill him. But if you can do anything, take pity on us and help us." [23] "'If you can'?" said Jesus. "Everything is possible for one who believes." [24] Immediately the boy's father exclaimed, "I do believe; **help me overcome my unbelief!**"* **Mark 9:17-24**

*[24] Now Thomas... one of the Twelve, was not with the disciples when Jesus came. [25] So the other disciples told him, "We have seen the Lord!" But he said to them, "Unless I see the nail marks in his hands and put my finger where the nails were, and put my hand into his side, I will not believe." [26] A week later his disciples were in the house again, and Thomas was with them. Though the doors were locked, Jesus came and stood among them and said, "Peace be with you!" [27] Then he said to Thomas, "Put your finger here; see my hands. Reach out your hand and put it into my side. **Stop doubting and believe.**"* **John 20:24-27**

How have you been made to believe that God can't handle your **waywardness**?

Contrary to your belief, God can handle your **waywardness**:

> *...This is what the Lord Almighty says: '**Return to me,**' declares the Lord Almighty, 'and I will return to you,' says the Lord Almighty.* **Zechariah 1:3**

> *But in their distress they turned to the Lord, the God of Israel, and sought him, and he was **found by them**.* **2 Chronicles 15:4**

> *³Then Jesus told them this parable: ⁴"Suppose one of you has a hundred sheep and loses one of them. Doesn't he leave the ninety-nine in the open country and go after the lost sheep until he finds it? ⁵And when he finds it, he joyfully puts it on his shoulders ⁶and goes home. Then he calls his friends and neighbors together and says, 'Rejoice with me; **I have found my lost sheep**.' ⁷I tell you that in the same way there will be more rejoicing in heaven over one sinner who repents than over ninety-nine righteous persons who do not need to repent.* **Luke 15:3-7**

How have you been made to believe that God can't handle your **weakness**?

Contrary to your belief, God can handle your **weakness**:

> *¹⁵"Pardon me, my lord," Gideon replied, "but how can I save Israel? My clan is the weakest in Manasseh, and I am the least in my family." ¹⁶The Lord answered, "**I will be with you**, and you will strike down all the Midianites, leaving none alive."* **Judges 6:15-16**

> *In the same way, the Spirit helps us in our weakness. We do not know what we ought to pray for, but **the Spirit himself intercedes for us** through wordless groans.* **Romans 8:26**

> *⁹But he said to me, "My grace is sufficient for you, for my power is made perfect in weakness." Therefore I will boast all the more gladly about my weaknesses, so that Christ's power may rest on me. ¹⁰That is why, for Christ's sake, I delight in weaknesses, in insults, in hardships, in persecutions, in difficulties. For when I am weak, **then I am strong**.* **2 Corinthians 12:9-10**

Let's re-frame what you believe God can handle.

Imagine handing everything you are afraid He can't handle back to Him. Take the time to write those things in the space provided.

My invitation to you is to take some time to tell God your whole truth, and by whole truth I mean coming before Him with all that you've got, all that comes out, all that your heart longs to say. The wounds, the fear, the anger, the past, the mistakes, the wrong-doings, the confusion, the contempt, and the hatred. Come to Him with your joy and your gratitude, your hope and your dreams. Lay it all out. No one is grading you. This is not a book report, a thesis paper, or something that will be judged. In fact, isn't that the whole thing... the bleeding woman came fully open, ready to be fully known by God, and it was in that moment she was fully freed.

This woman fell at Jesus' feet and told Him her whole truth, the good, the bad and the ugly and He could have responded in a million different ways... but look how He responds. Jesus calls her "Daughter." There is not a more personal name a Father can use than one that says, "You are mine. And I am yours." The Psalmist says, "*He determines the number of the stars and calls them each by name.*" **Psalm 147:4**

Our Father might call the stars by name,

but He calls you Daughter.

And when you come to Him fully vulnerable, fully transparent, with all the hurting messy parts exposed, it's then that He can make them whole. He can only make whole what you will allow Him to touch, to enter, to see. It will be then that you will be free.

Respond

Not only can God handle your whole truth, but He calls you daughter. Today, I encourage you to spend time thanking this Father who claims you as His own.

Counselor's Couch

Steve Call

One of Collide's core values is to recognize brokenness so it can be made whole. We have a growing community of women walking toward healing, as well as a community of counselors who are partnering with us to this end. We hope you not only enjoy hearing a counselor's voice here, but that you open yourself up to the transformational work God is calling you into so that you can see His healing as a reality in your life.

Adam and his wife were both naked, and they felt no shame. **Genesis 2:25**

Shame is deceptive. It creeps in uninvited. As I sat in a coffee shop, waiting for an older friend, I felt vulnerable. I had asked him to help me navigate the journey of marriage and parenting. To ask another man for help was not a common experience for me. I was taught to be self-sufficient, to not need help. As I waited, I began to feel anxious… nervous… agitated… distressed… I wanted to hide. I wanted to disappear. This was the third time in a row he did not show. Shame whispered, "You are not important. You are forgotten. You are unworthy. You are too needy…You are weak…You do not matter." What has shame been whispering to you?

For most of us, our shame whisper can become our shame dialogue. It's the messages we say secretly to ourselves; the silent but loud words we speak to ourselves about our shortcomings, failures, and inadequacies. These words are rooted in feeling unworthy, unlovable, not wanted. Shame tempts us to believe that at our core, we can't measure up; that we simply aren't enough.

Brene Brown is one of my heroes. She has done remarkable work on the topic of shame. She defines shame as "the intensely painful feeling or experience of believing that we are flawed and therefore unworthy of love and belonging… unworthy of connection." Most of our whispers of shame are kept secret and hidden. Sometimes our secrets become our truth. Shame whispers, "Do not tell." Shame whispers, "You must hide."

Then the man and his wife heard the sound of the Lord… and they hid… **Genesis 3:8**

We are not alone in our attempt to hide. Adam and Eve were tempted by their own desire, ate from the forbidden tree, felt shame and attempted to hide. Adam and Eve hid from God because they felt unworthy. In the coffee shop, I wanted to hide so that no one could see my shame. I am terrified of exposing my shame. I am terrified of exposing my shame to God. I am afraid that I am unworthy. I am afraid that He will turn away from me because I don't matter. Yet, hiding in my shame gives me the illusion of protection. Hiding is a form of temptation. Perhaps my fears keep me from turning to God when I feel shame. Perhaps your fears keep you from turning to God when you feel shame.

"…Where are you?" **Genesis 3:9**

There is another whisper though. It is the whisper of the Lord asking me, "Where are you?" His question is not out of judgment, condemnation or with the intent to harm, or hurt me. His whisper of, "Where are you?" is about a desire to protect me from my shame. His whisper is about a desire to protect you from your shame. Shame's whisper longs to convince me I am unworthy, unloved and forgotten. His whisper says you are worthy. You are loved. You belong to me. Shame's desire is to create disconnection. His desire is to create a connection.

…He came to his senses… **Luke 15:17**

Shame also disorients us and confuses us. I feel lost when I hear the whisper of shame. The story of the Prodigal Son is a scandalous story. It is a shocking story. The son takes his inheritance, squanders all his money, and becomes lost in his shame. Perhaps in hearing the whisper of shame, he also heard the whisper of his Father, "Where are you?" Because in the story we read that he "came to his senses." When I am lost in the whisper of my shame, the truth of the Father's whisper helps me to "come to my senses." I am invited to return home. I am reminded of who I am. He longs to wipe away the judgment. He longs to wipe away the fear. He longs to drown out the whisper of shame.

…But while he was still a long way off, his father saw him and was filled with compassion for him; he ran to his son… **Luke 15:20**

The father celebrates the return of his son with an embrace, with a celebration. He gifts him with shoes, sandals and a ring. The father welcomed his son home with open arms. He wiped away the whisper of shame. Perhaps God the Father is asking each of us, "Where are you?" Just as for Adam and Eve, He longs for us to come out of our hiding, fall into His embrace and tune our ears to His whisper of truth instead of the whisper of shame.

One of my favorite pictures is Rembrandt's portrayal of "Return of the Prodigal Son." It hangs in my office. The painting reveals the son kneeling before his father. The focus of the painting is the father's embrace of his son, reminding us of God's embrace as we return home. It is an embrace of compassion. It is an embrace of mercy. It is a stunning picture because it reminds me that the father's love for his son was based on the relationship with his son, not the performance of his son. In the midst of his pain, suffering, agony, and betrayal, the father not only welcomed him home but also embraced his son. Stunning and surprising.

When our family member, friend, co-worker, partner or spouse returns "home" from being lost in shame's grip, you and I can choose a response similar to the father's. We are invited to set aside, at least temporarily, the pain, suffering, and heartache and embrace the one who has returned.

Not only do we have a choice to turn away from our shame and return to the other, we have a choice to receive and embrace the one returning from the grip of shame. The father celebrates the return of his son with an embrace; an embrace that reveals tenderness, kindness, and compassion. Even a sense of empathy. Shame's antidote according to Brene Brown is empathy. When we respond to another out of empathy, shame simply loses its grip. When I set aside my own judgment and allow empathy to be offered, shame's whisper is silenced.

A Faith
That Heals 9

personal &
powerful

Read

²¹*When Jesus had again crossed over by boat to the other side of the lake, a large crowd gathered around him while he was by the lake.* ²²*Then one of the synagogue leaders, named Jairus, came, and when he saw Jesus, he fell at his feet.* ²³*He pleaded earnestly with him, "My little daughter is dying. Please come and put your hands on her so that she will be healed and live."* ²⁴*So Jesus went with him. A large crowd followed and pressed around him.* ²⁵*And a woman was there who had been subject to bleeding for twelve years.* ²⁶*She had suffered a great deal under the care of many doctors and had spent all she had, yet instead of getting better she grew worse.* ²⁷*When she heard about Jesus, she came up behind him in the crowd and touched his cloak,* ²⁸*because she thought, "If I just touch his clothes, I will be healed."* ²⁹*Immediately her bleeding stopped and she felt in her body that she was freed from her suffering.* ³⁰*At once Jesus realized that power had gone out from him. He turned around in the crowd and asked, "Who touched my clothes?"* ³¹*"You see the people crowding against you," his disciples answered, "and yet you can ask, 'Who touched me?'"* ³²*But Jesus kept looking around to see who had done it.* ³³*Then the woman, knowing what had happened to her, came and fell at his feet and, trembling with fear, told him the whole truth.* ³⁴*He said to her, "Daughter, your faith has healed you. Go in peace and be freed from your suffering."* **Mark 5:21-34**

Jesus said something to this woman that was so fascinating. He said, *"Your faith has healed you."* Over and over again as I collide with Jesus, I see Him being so delighted when people participate in their own healing. I don't think this is because we actually have the ability to "heal" ourselves. I think what God desires is that we would be a people who don't just sit around wanting, waiting, hoping, and claiming belief, all the while doing nothing. So often we have such high hopes for things to get better in our lives and yet we fail to engage the work God is calling us into to walk toward health.

Walk toward health!

It's so easy to wait for the miracle and in the meantime eat Cheetos and drink red wine and repress all the anxious thoughts, ignoring the prompt you had to start counseling. It's so easy to put your hope in the degree, the promotion, the award, or the accolade and not walk in the direction you need to go to get there. It's so easy to have a festering health condition and not call the doctor but hope it just somehow goes away.

I think Jesus wants us to walk toward health. That's what we say a lot around Collide. We invite women to walk toward health, don't just wait for health to walk toward you. Walking toward health requires our yes; God's invitation is waiting upon it. If you have baggage, don't just wait for God to come down from Heaven and miraculously lift your bags- journey with Him backwards to where you picked them up in the first place. That's the kind of work our God wants to do in all of our lives. He wants to walk with you toward healing. Don't just wait to win the lottery so you can pay off your debt, get a job and start chiseling away. Don't just pray for the life you hope to live, show up every day and lean into the work of getting it.

I just think Jesus wants us to participate in our own life, healing and dreams. He wants us to care, to have passion, to process, to feel, to work, to pick up the phone and call for help instead of expecting help to show up at our door.

Ruminate

Look up the following Scriptures where Jesus delighted in people's participation in their own lives, hopes and healing, and make notes on how they participated with God in the box below.

Passage of Scripture	Person	How they participated
Matthew 8:5-13	Centurion	came to Jesus asking for help
Matthew 9:27-31		
Mark 2:1-12		
Mark 7:24-30		
Luke 17:11-19		
John 5:1-12		

How do you sometimes wait on God for healing and wholeness instead of saying yes to God's invitation to walk toward health?

How do you think God is calling you to participate in your own life, health and dreams?

What kind of faith did the woman in **Mark 5** have that God honored it with a healing?

What does Jesus' statement, "your faith has healed you," imply for you and me?

I have Thought a lot about the kind of faith this woman had. It's not that she "saved" herself. Let me remind us that **Ephesians 2:8** says *"For it is by grace you have been saved, through faith—and this is not from yourselves, it is the gift of God."* We cannot save ourselves. As much as we try, we can't seem to throw ourselves a buoy when we are the ones drowning. We can't seem to sacrifice enough to make that nasty guilt that calls us nasty names go away. As much as we try to heal ourselves with tropical vacations and essential oils, big parties, fancy houses and lots of likes on Insta- none of that saves all the pain, all the abuse, all the skeletons in our closet. As much as we'd like to save ourselves, we need Someone bigger than us, mightier than us, more divine than us, smarter than us, and stronger than us. God is our Rescuer and our Salvation. It is by faith that we hand Him over our lives, expecting Him to rescue us once, as well as over and over again. As we do, we are saved, now and for eternity.

James 2:17 says, *"faith by itself, if it is not accompanied by action, is dead."* This might seem confusing but it's actually so, so great and here's why: this is God's way of doing away with all the hypocritical, white-washed, religious posing pansies who want to hide behind their profession of faith without having to look like Jesus at all. You know the kinds of people that drive you cray-cray. Jesus loved seeing people who professed faith in God AND looked like God. True faith transforms real life. True faith grasps so tightly to the teachings of Jesus Christ that even in the face of temptation to choose self, one must choose their neighbor. True faith is so convicted by the call to truth, that it cannot turn its back on God and lie to man. True faith holds so strongly to the character of God that it cannot but come falling at Jesus' feet, expecting Him to do something only He can do. True faith is always seen acting upon what it puts its hope in.

The bleeding woman's faith healed her not because she did anything to heal herself, but because of who she put her faith in. She put her faith in Jesus. She had faith to act upon what she believed. And here's what that faith looked like in action…

She had faith by showing up to hope.

Some of us gave up hoping in better health. We gave up hoping in safe friendships. We gave up hoping in meaningful work. We gave up hoping to be treated the way we deserve. We gave up hoping we could use our talents. We gave up hoping in our marriages.

It's time we show up to hope.

She had faith by redefining strength.

The thing that kills me about this collision is that the bleeding woman could have kept it all to herself in that crowd. She could have stayed strong and held her need for help in for everyone else, including the sick girl. But she chose to not to be alone at the risk of looking weak. That's strength. The strongest women I know can say, "I'm not okay. I need something I don't have." It's in our moments of surrender that true strength is born.

We need to redefine strength, and it's then we'll experience power.

She had faith by reaching out and grabbing hold of power before she could see it.

She couldn't see the healing, the freedom, or the life she wanted before she reached out and grabbed hold of it. We're waiting for God to show us the miracle, the plan, the happy ending before we grab hold of Him for it. That's not faith in God. That's faith in what we can see. This woman had faith in what she couldn't. It was when she reached for a power she could not see that she actually saw it. God's power is all around us but I'm afraid we're missing it because we are waiting to see it.

We don't see it until we reach out and grab hold of it.

Reflect

How do you need to show up to hope right now in your life?

As you've had more time to think about it, how do you need to continue to redefine strength?

Why do you think we are waiting to see the miracle, the good news, the answered prayer, the definitive path, the "power," before we reach out and grab hold of it?

I think we've misconstrued the definition of faith. Faith is not checking a box that says "Christian." Faith is not a "club" you belong to. Faith is not just aligning with some people you have some things in common with. Faith is not a bargaining chip. Faith is not safe. Faith is not easy. Faith is not something you choose only when things are hunky dory and you can see God's goodness all around you. Faith is not, "I will only like you God if you do what I'm asking." Faith is not, "I will only reach out to you if this goes the way I want it to." **Hebrews 11: 1** defines for us **faith:**

Now faith is confidence in what we hope for and assurance about what we do not see.

Reflect

Based on this definition of faith, take some time to think about what **faith is not** and what **faith is.**

Faith is not:	Faith is:
a guarantee	trust despite

Respond

God will honor your faith. Spend some time reaching out to God in faith knowing that He frees those who do.

Counselor's Couch

Kellie Furlan

One of Collide's core values is to recognize brokenness so it can be made whole. We have a growing community of women walking toward healing, as well as a community of counselors who are partnering with us to this end. We hope you not only enjoy hearing a counselor's voice here, but that you open yourself up to the transformational work God is calling you into so that you can see His healing as a reality in your life.

The faith-filled life of the Christian cannot be lived without taking risk. The Old and New Testaments are full of stories in which God asks people to do things that require stepping outside their comfort zones. Whether He's asking someone to literally leave with the shirt on their back and haul off to the desert towards a land they did not know or whether He's commanding us to not be conformed to the pattern of this world, God repeatedly invites His beloved into a life of abundance that is only possible if we are willing to risk for it.

So often, our "always" and "never" way of thinking keeps us from taking risks. The words "always" and "never" are two words that are unbudging, unyielding – they don't give way. They restrict. They are so permanent. And if you are talking about the character of God… always and never are rightly applied! He will never leave you. He has always been and will always be. Nothing can separate you from His love!

But when we are talking about our problems, our dilemmas, and our struggles, a limiting view is not helpful. A mindset of "always" and "never" short-cuts our thinking in ways that leave us shackled to the very things we are desperate to be free from. Rather than having our minds open and receptive to new information, looking at possibility, and using our sanctified imaginations… we stick with what we know.

For example, we might tell ourselves:

> I'll <u>never</u> be able to express my emotions.
>
> I'll <u>never</u> make friends.
>
> People are <u>never</u> safe.

I'll <u>always</u> be in physical pain.

I'll <u>always</u> feel this grief.

I'll <u>never</u> hear God's voice.

I'll <u>always</u> be damaged goods.

I'll <u>never</u> succeed.

The trouble with sticking with what we know is that we close our eyes to very important details about life and our scripts for living fail to update. We fail to see what Narrative Therapist's call unique outcomes – these are moments that defy the rule. They are outlier moments. They are unique not because they truly are unique, but because we ordinarily fail to acknowledge them because they fall outside what we expect. These are the moments when someone proved safe and trustworthy, moments when you had a bit of success, had a moment of friendship or were able to notice something besides the emptiness that a loss has left you with. These unique outcomes… outcomes that defy the always/never rule require noticing. And noticing unique outcomes might require more practice than you think.

Our core beliefs about ourselves, about the world, and about what God is like, operate at a subconscious level. Our vulnerability to this flaw of filtering the facts of our lives in ways that support our subconscious core beliefs is called "confirmation bias". Confirmation bias is the tendency to only pay attention to information that confirms what we already think, believe or expect.

Are you willing to look at the evidence that turns "always" and "never" into "sometimes" and "on occasion"? And if you discover evidence that contradicts your limiting beliefs about yourself, God or the world, are you willing to face what has become comfortable about your problem-saturated story and risk walking away from it into the life Jesus is calling you into? What would be the first step of courage that you would need to take?

I challenge you to start paying attention to the tiny evidences that disprove faulty notions about yourself, God or the world. If your problem is that people are unsafe I want you to start noticing every safe interaction you have with a human and think about what you might have to face if only some people are unsafe.

We know that our early understandings of ourselves, others and God stick with us long after we originally develop them – and we know it takes a lot of evidence to bring what we know in our hearts in congruence with what we know in our heads. So why not get going, start amassing the evidence.

It's risky business updating those core beliefs, otherwise we'd do it more readily. Somehow, those core beliefs however limiting they are, are protecting us from something. It's your job to figure out what that something is, and to seriously consider if you are willing to face what your always/never thinking is protecting you from. It might be just this place where God is calling you into the abundant life He has for you.

Missing Power

personal & powerful

I was in a plane crash the same year I handed my life to God. My boyfriend was the pilot. Our plane went down in the San Juan Islands. We lost one wing and all the wheels. That should have been my goodbye… but there was that one wing. Upon our descent, that one wing got caught dangling in some trees, which saved the nose from impact on its way down. And you know what? I missed the power. For 25 years I've said, "I was in plane crash," but I think I missed that I was in a "rescue mission."

> We often don't see the power
> when we have to go through the pain.

When my daughter Bella was about three years old she got a fever. After a few days, I made an appointment to go to the doctor. I don't know about you but I avoid doing this because I hate waiting for hours to hear, "If the fever persists for a few more days, give us a call. That will be 349 dollars." But that's exactly what happened. Five days later, Bella still had a 105 degree temperature with no other symptoms, so I called back.

I was partially motivated to call because I found a penny in her poop. You know, you would have a lot more money if you would sort through your kids' diapers. I saw the poopy penny and thought, "Maaaaaybe that's why she has a fever." Our general doc wasn't working when I went in the second time, and it turns out she didn't take notes from our first visit, so her sub doc started to do that thing…"If the fever persists for a few more days…" He was going to send me home to wait a few more days since he had no records. My girl only had a fever and he probably wrote me off as a worry wart. Something I said and something he thought made him second guess his own advice and he ordered a blood test. He assured me eating pennies doesn't cause fevers and they'd call in a day or two with the results. Within hours my phone rang and the doctor told me to go to the hospital right way, a room was waiting for Bella.

When we arrived, a doctor came in and asked us the story that led up to the hospital stay. He said Bella had bacteria in her blood that could travel to her brain and if that happens, it could be bad, even fatal. For a few days, we agonized and prayed while they administered hardcore medicine to fight the infection. The doctor came back and told us that Bella was turning around and was going to be okay! Then he said very seriously, "If you would have come in here even two days later, this would have been a different story." God saved my baby but I missed seeing the power because it had come two days earlier when I didn't even know I needed it. We don't see power when it comes early. We don't see power when it comes late...

We only see power when it comes when and how we want it to.

I once experienced a terrible arm injury that left me walking in search of help, holding up a mangled arm because it couldn't hold itself up. My kids and I walked from the beach toward the nearest road so the ambulance could find me. So many people passed by as I searched for the medics and not one stopped to help. I was trying to be strong for my kids but I was about to vomit or pass out so I sat down on a bench and prayed. I asked God for one thing: "Please just bring by one person in this town I know."

My kids were freaking out, our bikes were left at the beach, and I was in utter pain. My elbow bone had been impacted by a 400 pound boulder. It had popped out and up, about as far as it could go. I found out later that the medics thought I was on the other side of the park, so I sat on that bench in agony for a very long time waiting, hoping that each person that passed might be someone I knew. And no one I knew came. I mean how hard is it to answer that prayer?

By the time I got to the emergency room, I was in such bad pain that all I wanted to do was scream, "Give meeeee drugs!" But I figured if I did that they might think I have a drug problem. So I tried to play it cool like I didn't want drugs... to get drugs. The wait was long because people were coming in from fatal car accidents and heart attacks. They wheeled me in for an x-ray and wouldn't you know it, on my way out I passed by someone I knew. She was an ER nurse who had spoken at a Collide conference. She called my name and came after me. She wasn't working that day but happened to be visiting her co-workers. She immediately picked up her magical phone that got me drugs and doctors within minutes. The five medical staff surrounding me said, "We're gonna give you Michael Jackson drugs," and I said, "I'm gonna need you to turn me back on." And they said, "We're gonna give you something so you never remember the pain you're about to feel." And I said, "When are you gonna reset my arm?" And they said, "We already did."

We miss God's power because it doesn't come how we expect it to, but it comes how we need it most.

Reflect

You know why the bleeding woman came to Jesus? Go back and re-read **Mark 5:21-43**. What led this woman to come and collide with Jesus?

The Bible says she heard about Jesus. We too have heard about Jesus and His power. What have you heard about Jesus' power? Take some time to write down the rumors about His power:

Jesus has the power to calm the sea
Jesus has the power to cast out demons
Jesus has the power to turn water into wine

There are only two ways to live your life. One is as though **nothing** is a miracle.

The other is as though **everything** is a miracle. - Albert Einstein

You and I have heard that the God whose power sculpted the heavens, the Big Dipper and the Milky Way, also restored a man with deformed hands. We've heard that the God whose power made Earth and all that is in it, including Ryan Gosling, your beautiful children, Hawaii, Mt. Everest and pomegranates, He also made a meal for 5,000 out of one boy's measly lunch (and we crafted a whole Bible study, called Yes, You around it… visit wecollide.net for details). We've heard that the God whose power sent frogs, gnats, flies, boils, hail, blood, and more to let His people go, also sent demons out of a demon-possessed man to free him. We've heard that the God whose power spoke a word in the beginning and there was light, He also spoke the word, "Go," to a blind man who went seeing that light. We've heard that this Jesus was put to death on a cross, but by His power death could not hold Him down, and He promised us this same power. In fact, it's all around us.

There is a quote, often attributed to Albert Einstein that says, "There are only two ways to live your life. One is as though nothing is a miracle. The other is as though everything is a miracle."

Is it not power that no matter where you are on this planet, we all see the same moon? *Is it not power* that gravitational pull which you cannot see is what grounds your labradoodle, your house, your Prius, and your body to stay here on Earth? *Is it not power,* that "pull" is what causes Earth to take a lap around the sun and without it we'd likely crash right into that hot radiating nuclear reacting ball of gases? *Is it not power* that your heart beats 100,000 times a day, pumping about 2,000 gallons of blood to blood vessels in your body that if laid end to end would measure 60,000 miles? *Is it not power* that something the size of a blueberry can have eyelids and become your baby girl eight months later? *Is it not power* that the brain itself doesn't have any pain receptors, which is what makes it possible to perform brain surgery on people while they're awake? *Is it not power* that your brain can recall 50,000 different scents, including the ones I am about to mention…

fresh-baked chocolate chip cookies
a rose
dog poo

Is it not power that two broken human beings can stay together, even though after 20 years they can't compromise over the direction the toilet paper should hang? *Is it not power* that there is the caterpillar and the butterfly, because without the caterpillar, how cool would a butterfly really be? *Is it not power* when you are saved by one wing dangling in trees, a doctor going against his own advice, and an ER nurse not on shift? *Is it not power* that the tulip comes popping out of the ground every spring, reminding us that resurrection is possible after death?

For further study on *God's power,* check out the resource page at wecoolide.net

All I know is that if you haven't seen God's power yet, it's near and you better not miss reaching out and grabbing hold of it because you're too busy telling it that it's too late, too early or not just how you ordered it with a fried egg and wheat toast.

Sometimes power comes on the other side of grief, even though power is what got you through. Sometimes power comes six chapters after the chapter that had you walking down the road, all alone, waiting for your dad to come. And though you can only see the power six chapters later, it was always there, just like the stars. Sometimes power comes on the other side of winter, in spring. And sometimes it comes when you reach out and grab hold of it, even though you can't see it and it's then that you will.

Reflect

How has pain made it hard for you to see God's power?

How have you missed power because it came too early (like before you knew you needed it)? Or too late (like after you had hoped for it)?

How have you missed power because it showed up and didn't look the way you expected it to?

How do you sometimes "order up" God's power like you're telling a waiter what you want for breakfast?

When you think about the idea that everything is a miracle and power is all around you, what are some things you can think of right now that point you to God's power?

How are you challenged by the idea that power comes when you reach out and grab hold of it, even though you can't see it, and it's then, that you will?

Respond

As we have been talking about, sometimes we miss power even though it's right in front of us. Sometimes we miss miracles even though they're all around us. I encourage you to respond by making space in the next few days to go be somewhere you cannot escape God's power. Go sit on the edge of the ocean and be overwhelmed by how big God is. Go watch an Imax film with your kids that shows you the intricacy of the creatures of the sea in a way that you can't help but be in awe of your Creator. Go for a walk on a trail and note the changing of the leaves or the budding of a cherry tree, immersing yourself in the presence of God who brings forth all seasons. Sit in it. Walk in it. Ponder and take it in. God's power is in the thunder and it's right there in the NICU. God's power is in your favorite people's smiles and it's also evident as you soak your feet in the sand on the shore. Don't miss it... go looking for it this week and then respond to God as your heart so leads you.

Faith or Fear?

personal & powerful

Read

³³Then the woman, knowing what had happened to her, came and fell at his feet and, trembling with fear, told him the whole truth. ³⁴He said to her, "Daughter, your faith has healed you. Go in peace and be freed from your suffering." ³⁵While Jesus was still speaking, some people came from the house of Jairus, the synagogue leader. "Your daughter is dead," they said. "Why bother the teacher anymore?" ³⁶Overhearing what they said, Jesus told him, "Don't be afraid; just believe."
Mark 5:33-36

Jesus stopped for this woman on His way somewhere important. Because Jesus stopped for this one woman, it cost Jairus' daughter her life.

Reflect

If you were on your way somewhere really, really important, how likely would it be that you would stop because someone "touched" your clothes?

How do you think Jairus is feeling right about now about Jesus? About this woman?

How do you think this woman probably felt to know that God stopped for her and then this man's daughter died?

What do you think is the significance that Jesus called this woman He stopped for "daughter" and now the "daughter" Jesus was on his way to see just died because He stopped?

When we see God stop for other people, how does it feel when we don't feel like He's stopping for us?

What encourages you about the idea that God stopped for her and that God stops for you?

Jesus told Jairus, *"Don't be afraid; just believe."* Jesus knows that we each have *two voices.* We have a voice of Fear and we have a voice of Faith. Fear tells you it's a done deal and Faith tells you redemption's on its way. Fear keeps you up at night, Faith says God's got this. Fear tries to knock you down, Faith fights to get you back up. Fear says stay safe, Faith says move. Fear tells you God doesn't know what He's doing, Faith reminds you what He's doing is always greater than what we think He ought to. Faith counts on the resurrection even in the agony of goodbye. Faith holds onto hope no matter how ridiculous, irrational or illogical hope might look.

Women with faith say, "My God, He is coming. If He hasn't come, He will. He is on His way, He knows when, He knows how, He knows why and He knows best."

Don't be afraid; just believe. Mark 5:36b

Who is bossing you around?

Take some time to think about what your fear and your faith are telling you right now and write those statements down in the table below:

Fear	Faith
Don't waste your time hoping this will change!	God makes all things new!

It is so easy to let our Fear boss us around. Imagine all the things we let Fear tell us to do. We let Fear tell us… "Don't take any risks in case you fail. Don't pray for that, agaaaain, you've asked a million times. Don't get your hopes up. Don't put yourself out there. Don't keep bothering God." You can keep letting Fear's voice boss you around or you can allow Faith to tell you what to do. It's up to you. That's the beauty. You get to choose whose voice you allow to be louder.

For a woman's conference we crafted, our Collide team wrote a monologue depicting one woman's two voices: Fear and Faith. We had it recorded just for you. You can find it at wecollide.net/i-am-still-the-girl-podcast/. After you listen, let's reflect.

Reflect

How do you see the difficult life experiences of the woman in the podcast beginning to inform her hope?

What has she gone through that messes with her faith?

How do you see Fear and Faith colliding?

Why do you think Fear is often so much louder than Faith?

How have you allowed yourself to believe that your fears actually protect you from disappointment and getting hurt even more?

This woman in the podcast says, "I lost my daughter and when I lost her, God lost me..." How do you relate?

What advice would you give your 10 year old self, knowing what lies ahead, about the power of the voices Fear and Faith?

Reread your own advice. How do these words minister to you today?

Jairus was a man of faith. In fact, it was faith that led Jairus to come to Jesus in the first place, but it was his circumstances that began to weaken that faith. How have you seen circumstances weaken your faith, or someone's else's around you?

What do circumstances often tell your faith?

Have you ever thought about coming to God with the thing you are worried about, the thing you want changed, the thing you need a miracle for and thought, "Why bother God? He didn't do anything to keep this from being a need…"?

Jairus had witnessed Jesus' power heal the woman and now Jesus is calling him to have her same kind of faith. Maybe this is why she was healed when she was, and not any other time during the last 11 years and 364 days. Maybe her story was a part of a greater story. Maybe her story was a part of bringing healing to more than her own life… to the crowd, the community, Jairus, and his daughter… As we are about to see, because Jairus got to see Jesus' power in the bleeding woman's life, maybe he was able to believe it for his own.

Reflect

What strikes you about the idea that your story is part of a greater story and if that be true, when and how God chooses to heal you has to do with you AND so many other people?

If Jesus would have come right away to heal the father's daughter, would the father's perspective of Jesus have been different, and if so, how?

Keep in mind Jairus' hopes are absolutely crushed. Everything he wanted and came to Jesus hoping for, just got dashed. His daughter, the sweet love of his life, is now gone and Jesus seemed to have control over how fast He could have arrived on her scene. And YET, Jesus doesn't respond to Jairus by saying:

> "Yeah, it's too late."
> "Sorry, I got busy."
> "What's done is done."
> "Move on."
> "This is how your story goes."
> "Something else came up."

"It is what it is."

"You're going to have to deal with the cards you were dealt."

"It's not about what you wanted- this is your reality."

"I meant to but I got distracted."

"Yep, you're the one in the story that doesn't get what you want."

"You didn't quite make the cut to deserving your miracle."

Let's stop for a second. Go back through the things Jesus could have said to Jairus. How often do you start believing these kinds of statements? Circle the ones you resonate most with and sense God is saying when you don't get what you have hoped and prayed and pleaded for.

Jesus doesn't say any of those things! Jesus says, *"Don't be afraid; just believe."* His daughter is dead. She is gone. There's no getting her back. Jairus' friends would never come and tell him that kind of news, if they weren't sure. And Jesus had the audacity to say, "Just believe." How do you feel when someone says, "Just have faith," in the face of death, grief, or a story ending earlier than you wanted it to?

Jairus has a choice. And so do we. God gives us the ability to choose every day, all day, will we fear or will we believe? We might not be able to choose our circumstances, but we can choose how we respond to them.

Viktor E. Frankl, in <u>Man's Search for Meaning</u> said, "Everything can be taken from a man but one thing: the last of the human freedoms—to choose one's attitude in any given set of circumstances, to choose one's own way."[11]

11 Frankl, Viktor E. Man's Search for Meaning. Export ed edition ed., Rider, 2008.

Respond

Today I don't doubt that you face a circumstance, a hardship or a decision where you are having to choose Fear or Faith. No matter where you find yourself, I am going to hold out Faith for you, in case you can't hold it for yourself. Sometimes that's what we do for each other as women. Sometimes we have to hold belief up for each other's hopes. So read this prayer that I pray for you as we close…

God,

We come to you in Faith, and even if our Faith has been making friends with Doubt and Fear, we are gonna choose Faith. We are gonna be women who say, "I know you have a plan. I know you can make a way. I know you know what you are doing. And no matter how much Fear is trying to bring me down and convince me you don't know what you're doing — I'm going to choose to believe that you do." In the same way you stop for others, we are going to believe you stop for us. We are going to audaciously believe that you are going to do what we can't imagine, see, understand or comprehend. We, by faith, choose to believe you are personal and powerful, right in the face of feeling forgotten and weak. You ask us to choose Faith, Jesus, so we will. Eradicate our fear. Make your voice louder than all fear's bossy commands. Make fear go away and instead replace it with trust, pure nonsensical trust.

We pray this in God's powerful and personal name, Jesus,

Amen.

The Story's Not Over

personal &
powerful

Read

35While Jesus was still speaking, some people came from the house of Jairus, the synagogue leader. "Your daughter is dead," they said. "Why bother the teacher anymore?" 36Overhearing what they said, Jesus told him, "Don't be afraid; just believe." 37He did not let anyone follow him except Peter, James and John the brother of James. 38When they came to the home of the synagogue leader, Jesus saw a commotion, with people crying and wailing loudly. 39He went in and said to them, "Why all this commotion and wailing? The child is not dead but asleep." 40But they laughed at him. After he put them all out, he took the child's father and mother and the disciples who were with him, and went in where the child was. 41He took her by the hand and said to her, "Talitha koum!" (which means "Little girl, I say to you, get up!"). 42Immediately the girl stood up and began to walk around (she was twelve years old). At this they were completely astonished. 43He gave strict orders not to let anyone know about this, and told them to give her something to eat. **Mark 5:35-43**

This is a scene, a devastating, hard, no-one-should-ever-have-to-experience-this kind of scene. I have had this experience before. It's one of the worst things I have ever, ever, ever had to watch a family walk through. This kind of loss blindsides you, messes with all your theology and no amount of "religious" answers bring peace. The lights turn off and stay that way for a very long time. Bitterness has the great potential to take root and bloom. No amount of blessing you experienced before this moment talks you into getting out of bed and trying to see light and "do" joy.

Jesus walked into this kind of scene where people were full fledged mourning the loss of a child. They even called in the professionals. In this culture, people actually hired professional mourners who came in and wailed for you so that when you ran out of energy to wail and lament and mourn, they did it for you. And Jesus walks in and has the audacity to say, "*…the child is not dead but asleep.*" Of course those present laughed at the ridiculousness of such a statement. Pro mourners know death when they see it. That's their job.

The story is never over.

With Jesus,

Jesus went into where she lay, took her by the hand and said, *"Little girl, I say to you, get up!"* And you know what? This twelve year old girl who died, stood up and walked.

In that moment when Jesus gave her life, He knew what would happen to His.

The Bible says they were astonished. They were astonished because they were living as though the story was over. Some of us live like our story is over in our

marriage,
body,
career,
diagnoses,
dreams.

We live like the story ends in death, but it ends in resurrection. The same thing Jesus did for this girl, He will do for us. He will show Himself to be powerful and personal in our lives even to the very end, and even then again.

See with Jesus, the story is never over.[12]

12 Cole, R. A. (1994). Mark. In D. A. Carson, R. T. France, J. A. Motyer, & G. J. Wenham (Eds.), New Bible commentary: 21st century edition (4th ed., p. 960). Leicester, England; Downers Grove, IL: Inter-Varsity Press.

How are you living like the story is already over?

When you think about the idea that with Jesus the story is never over, how does that encourage you in the chapter you currently find yourself?

Where do you need a resurrection?

How does the idea that even when you think it's the end, the very end, with Jesus it's still not over?

Ruminate

Read the following Scriptures that assure us that with Jesus, the story is never over, and claim their truths by filling in the blanks.

⁵As they entered the tomb, they saw a young man dressed in a white robe sitting on the right side, and they were alarmed. ⁶"Don't be alarmed," he said. "You are looking for Jesus the Nazarene, who was crucified. He has risen! He is not here. See the place where they laid him. ⁷But go, tell his disciples and Peter, 'He is going ahead of you into Galilee. There you will see him, just as he told you.'" **Mark 16:5-7**

The _____tomb_____ is not the end of the story.

⁶"He is not here; he has risen! Remember how he told you, while he was still with you in Galilee: ⁷'The Son of Man must be delivered over to the hands of sinners, be crucified and on the third day be raised again.'" **Luke 24:6-7**

The crucifixion is not the _____ chapter.

Jesus said to her, "I am the resurrection and the life. The one who believes in me will live, even though they die." **John 11:25**

Jesus was not only resurrected, He Himself is the _____ .

By his power God raised the Lord from the dead, and he will raise us also. **1 Corinthians 6:14**

By the same _____ Jesus was raised, you and I will be raised.

Praise be to the God and Father of our Lord Jesus Christ! In his great mercy he has given us new birth into a living hope through the resurrection of Jesus Christ from the dead. **1 Peter 1:3**

The story is not over and so we have a living _____ .

⁸Now if we died with Christ, we believe that we will also live with him. ⁹For we know that since Christ was raised from the dead, he cannot die again; death no longer has mastery over him. ¹⁰The death he died, he died to sin once for all; but the life he lives, he lives to God. ¹¹In the same way, count yourselves dead to sin but alive to God in Christ Jesus. **Romans 6:8-11**

Death no longer has _____ over Jesus and death no longer has

_____ over you.

The story is not over with

cancer
a death certificate
divorce
miscarriage
the loss of a dream
public humiliation
betrayal
failure
addiction
bankruptcy
man's curse
a dark road
or unforgiveness...

With Jesus you can always count on **more**. You can always count on **power**. You can always count on **life**.

So you can always *hope*. Never lose *hope*. Never let someone else tell you the story is over. Never let depression determine the plot. Never let mess-ups tell you, "Why bother?" Never let one bad chapter write the rest. Never believe God's a no-show. Never grieve without belief.

> Your timeline is not God's.
> Your doubt is not gospel.
> Your fear is not prophetic.
> Your worry is not the boss.
> Your past is not your future.
> Your period placement is not the end.

Look, you can either be a woman who buys in with all she's got, that God truly has the power to resurrect what feels dead and what is dead, or you don't. Sure, it's radical. Sure, it's crazy. Sure, it seems impossible…but so does Jesus raising a twelve year old, and so does Jesus walking out of a tomb because of that same power and promising it to you and me.

Being a woman of *faith* believes that though you might not have gotten your healing, you will get your resurrection. Though you feel like your appeal was unmet, doesn't mean God isn't coming. Though you might not be able to see Him, doesn't mean He's not here. Though you doubt it's possible, doesn't mean you're right.

Though you feel like it's devastatingly over, that might just be grounds for a

Triumphant,
amazing,
powerful,
no way,
not possible,
life giving,
holy cow,
Jesus just showed up,
personally and powerfully,
doing what I never imagined,
right smack dab in my
greatest hour of need.

Respond

Pray this prayer with me today.

Oh Jesus the Resurrection, the One who brings life over and over and over again, bring life where I worry there's death and despair, sickness and worry, fear and what looks like closed chapters. God, by faith and in hope, I am counting on you to collide with my life and resurrect and redeem the stories I gave up on. God, I stopped showing up to hope and I started giving into the ways brokenness and sin try to put an end to things. No more, God. I want to buy into the truth that you bring back what is dead, you heal what is sick, you make possible what looks impossible. So, God, I'm turning in my whole story and my whole life and I'm choosing faith over fear. You, Jesus hold all the power I need. Resurrect my hope and my faith and help me to live every moment trusting you to be personal and powerful.

I pray this in the name of Jesus, who collides with hurting and sick women and girls and brings them healing and life.

Amen.

Leader Guide

friends!

I cannot express how much I think leading a group of women centering around a passage of scripture where Jesus collides, will change lives! Your sacrifice, investment, service and care of these women has the capacity to change their family lives, their friendships, their stress and anxiety, their dreams and their sense of purpose! We cannot wait to hear the ways Jesus collides with you and your gathering of women as you walk them through this study! We have tried to put together a 90-minute experience that you can walk women through each time you meet together, covering each part of the study. Please be prayerful, give yourself grace and feel free to cut, edit or add to the experience as you feel so led! If you hate a question we suggest, skip it. If you think of some fun engaging activity that will add to your group's experience, do it! We trust that God is leading you and we merely give you this leader's guide as a tool to use as you see best. May God collide with you as you invite others to collide with Him!

Section 1
Surrounded Yet All Alone

Supplies needed:
Collide Bible Study Book
Bible
Box of tissues

Leader (20 minutes)

Welcome!

Invite each woman to introduce herself by answering the following 3 questions:

- *What is your name?*
- *Why are you excited to be here?*
- *What is one unique thing about you, your personality, life experience or giftings? (Examples: I grew up living on a houseboat. Or I have a prosthetic leg. Or I speak 3 languages. Or I'm allergic to pineapple.)*

Group (55 minutes)

Activity

Hand out a tissue to each woman and complete the following exercise:

- *By engaging in this exercise, the hope is that you will allow yourself to be met with compassion and you will meet others with your compassion because you resonate with their experience and they with yours. I'm going to read some scenarios and if that experience rings true for you, I want you to raise your tissue and exchange it with someone else who has their tissue raised. When you exchange tissues, say some kind of compassionate statement to each other like, "I've been there," "I've cried over that too," or whatever organically rolls off your tongue. If only one of us raises a tissue after a certain scenario, let's all exchange tissues with that person and tell her, "I see you." OK, Let's start easy:*
  - *If any of you crushed on someone growing up who did not choose you, go ahead and raise your tissue.*
  - *If you have ever looked in the mirror and struggled with what you saw, raise your tissue.*

- *If you have experienced the devastating effects of alcoholism or drug addiction with family or friends, raise your tissue.*
- *If you have ever had to face the ugly, awful torture that is cancer in your own life, your families' or friends' lives, raise your tissue.*
- *If your life has ever experienced the mess and grief that comes from divorce or a painful break up, raise your tissue.*
- *If you had dreams for your life that have yet to come true, raise your tissue.*

- *Take a look around the room and know that we are profoundly surrounded by brave, strong, compassionate women who can genuinely say to us and us to them, "Me too. I get it. I've cried so many tears over that same thing," and we are surrounded by a God who meets us here.*
- *In doing this activity, what do you notice are some of the things we have in common?*
- *Call out some of the ways you find women comparing themselves with others.*

Read Mark 5:21-43
Reflect

- *What are some of the things from this passage of scripture that immediately jump out at you?*
- *What are some of the commonalities you see between the two women in the passage of scripture?*
- *Have you ever felt alone in a crowd and if so, describe the experience.*
- *How do you think the woman bleeding in the crowd must have felt surrounded yet all alone?*

Partner (5 minutes)

Reflect

- *Split into groups of 2 or 3 and discuss the various ways we often feel alone from pp. 17-18. Share with your partner(s) the one you resonate with the most and why.*

Leader (10 minutes)

Respond

- Pray aloud for the group, the prayer on p. 20 (change the pronouns to include the entire group).

Section 2
Redefining Strength

Supplies needed:
Collide Bible Study Book
Bible

Leader (10 minutes)

Welcome!

- *Last week we discussed how we sometimes feel alone, even when we are surrounded by others. Were there times this week you noticed yourself feeling that way? If so, did you remember the activity we did with the tissues and were you able to remind yourself that though it may not seem like it, other women often feel the same way?*

Partner (15 minutes)

Reflect

- *Split into groups of 2 or 3 and discuss ways you have defined strength in your own life and why you think you define strength that way.*

Group (30 minutes)

Read Mark 5:21-24
Reflect

- *Have you ever had an experience where what you were looking for was right in front of you but you missed it?*
- Discuss the questions about Jairus coming to Jesus on p. 26.

Ruminate

- Have several women read aloud the passages on pp. 27-28.
- *Which verse had the most meaning for you based on where you are in your life right now and why?*
- *What do these verses tell you about God's response to us when we come to Him in need and what feels like weakness?*

Partner (10 minutes)

Reflect

- Split into groups of 2 or 3 and share what "strong people" look like based on your new definitions of strength from p. 30.

Group (15 minutes)

Reflect

- How does this statement strike you: "It was because this strong, successful, independent, leader risked looking weak, and redefined strength, that he ended up seeing his daughter's life saved."
- What if Jairus would have stayed home because that's what "strong people" do?
- How are you "staying at home" right now in your life, trying to look strong, when what you really need to do is come to Jesus in your need and "weakness"?
- What do you need to let go of in order to redefine strength in your own life?
- What do you love about Jesus' response to Jairus when he came to Him for help?

Leader (10 minutes)

Respond

- Let's close today by redefining strength and being brave in coming before God. As we close in prayer together, I want each of us to say, out loud, "God, I am coming to you and asking you to help me with…"

Section 3
Impersonal and Weak

Supplies needed:
Collide Bible Study Book
Bible
Whiteboard or large piece of paper

Leader (10 minutes)

Welcome!

- *How did you see culture represent strength this week in what you saw on TV, social media, news or the movies?*
- *Did anyone have an opportunity this week to put some of our new definitions of strength into practice?*

Group (30 minutes)

Read Mark 5:24-26 and Leviticus 15:25-27
Reflect

- **Activity** – Use a whiteboard or large piece of paper to recreate the chart on p. 37. Have the group help you fill in the chart with the ways this woman would have been affected by being considered "unclean."
- *What would this experience begin to tell you about the possibility of a better outcome?*

Partner (20 minutes)

Reflect

- *Split into groups of 2 or 3 and share how you would feel if you were in this woman's position. (5 minutes)*
- *Read the paragraph on p. 39 together and discuss the reflection questions that follow on pp. 40-41. (15 minutes)*

Group (20 minutes)

Reflect

- *We need to be women who tell our circumstances who God is rather than allowing our circumstances to tell us who He is. What difficult circumstance in your life right now is telling you who God is?*
- *Let's allow our circumstances to be reminded who God is by reading Scripture that recalls His character as personal and powerful:* Have one woman read aloud the first group of scriptures that show how God is personal on p. 42.
- *Which of these verses did you need to hear the most and why?*
- Have one woman read aloud the second group of scriptures that show how God is powerful on pp. 42-43.
- *Which of these verses did you need to hear the most and why?*

Leader (10 minutes)

Respond

- *Ask women to share what they need to claim about God to their circumstances and incorporate those claims into your closing prayer.*

Section 4
Risk Hoping Again

Supplies needed:
Collide Bible Study Book
Bible

Leader (10 minutes)

Welcome!

- *What are some ways you noticed God showing up in your life in a personal or powerful way this week?*

Group (10 minutes)

Read Mark 5:25-28 and the following paragraph on p. 51
Reflect

- *Have you ever felt or seen someone else feel as though hoping would just bring about more disappointment?*
- *What strikes you about the idea of this woman reaching out and hoping in Jesus?*

Partner (10 minutes)

Reflect

- *Split into groups of 2 or 3 and discuss the reflection questions on p. 52.*

Group (30 minutes)

Reflect

- *Why is it sometimes difficult to believe a new outcome is possible?*
- *What amazes you about this woman who suffered for so long but somehow still came out believing a new outcome was possible for her?*
- *When you think about the woman whose dreams of being an actress and a mom were dashed and "her decision to no longer hope that a better outcome was possible was almost as painful as the circumstances that led her there"... how have you found that to be true when you give up hope?*

163

● *So, if not hoping has the capacity to leave us stuck and distant from God and hoping has the capacity to disappoint, what do you feel led to choose?*

Ruminate

● Read **Romans 5:5** over the group. *How does it encourage you that our hope will never be put to shame?*

Individual (5 minutes)

Reflect

● *Look at the answer you wrote on p. 56 about an area of your life where you have given up hoping for a different outcome. Spend some time expanding on your answer. What circumstances have led you to the place of giving up hope?*

Group (10 minutes)

Reflect

● Spend some time discussing the risk the woman took.

Individual (5 minutes)

Reflect

● *Look again at the answer you wrote on p. 56 and the circumstances that led you to that place. Now write one risk you can take to begin hoping again in this particular area or circumstance in your life.*

Leader (10 minutes)

Respond

● Ask women if they are willing to bravely share the risks they can take to begin believing in a new outcome. Have women pair up and pray with each other for the courage and strength to take a risk and begin hoping again.

● *Next week, bring an item that symbolizes something people turn to when they are looking for a cure for their ailments or a coping mechanism for their hardships. (Examples might be: Apple (to keep the doctor away) A trash magazine (to swim in the shallow), band aid (to cover wounds), a Web MD printout (to try and self diagnose), a bottle of red wine (to numb the pain), a credit card (for retail therapy).*

Section 5
If

Supplies needed:
Collide Bible Study Book
Bible
Whiteboard or large piece of paper
Item that symbolizes a cure for ailments and hardships

Leader (10 minutes)

Welcome!

- Have the group go around and share the object they brought that symbolizes something "people" turn to for a cure for their ailments or a coping mechanism for their hardships.

Group (45 minutes)

Read Mark 5:27-28
Reflect

- **Activity** – Have women call out their "if I just" statements from p. 63 and write them on the whiteboard or paper.
- *How do some of these "If I justs" actually make us worse off?*

Ruminate

- *Which of the people from the table on p. 65 do you resonate with the most and why?*
- *Does anyone want to bravely share how their "if I just" has left them worse off?*

Reflect

- Discuss the reflection questions on p. 66.

Ruminate

- Read **Daniel 3:1-30** and discuss:
    - *What is compelling about the response of Shadrach, Meshach and Abednego?*
    - *Why is this kind of "even if" faith so rarely exemplified?*

Partner (25 minutes)

Reflect

- *Discuss the reflection questions on pp. 68-69* (10 minutes)
- *Spend time sharing how you filled in the table on p. 70. Then, take some time to pray for one another about the "though I am's" on your partner's list and claim for them the "God is" statements.* (15 minutes).

Leader (10 minutes)

Respond

- Return to the list of "If I just" statements you wrote on the whiteboard and erase them or cross them out. Have the group call out the type of "even if" statements they hope to be able to claim. Write these statements instead.
- Pray over the women in your group that even in the midst of difficult circumstances, they will be able to say, "even if…. I will trust You."

Section 6
A Transaction

Supplies needed:
Collide Bible Study Book
Bible
Whiteboard or large piece of paper
Blank piece of paper for each woman

Leader (10 minutes)

Welcome!

- *Last week, we spent a lot of time talking about the concept of having a faith that says "even if." How did you find opportunities this week to adopt this mindset?*

Group (30 minutes)

Read Mark 5:29-30a and Isaiah 53:4-5
Reflect

- *What do you find interesting about the idea that a transaction occurred between this woman and Jesus?*

Ruminate

- **Activity** – Use the headings from the table on p. 78 to make a chart on the whiteboard. Have women call out the other examples they came up with or brainstorm together and write them in the chart.
- Discuss the 2 questions that follow the table on p. 79.

Partner (10 minutes)

Ruminate

- *Split into groups of 2 or 3 and read* **Isaiah 53:4-7** *together. Then discuss the next 4 questions on p. 81*

Group (10 minutes)

Read Matthew 27:27-50
Reflect

- *What does the cross tell you about Jesus' love, that is willing to transact your healing in exchange for His pain?*

Individual (10 minutes)

- **Activity** – Give each woman a blank piece of paper and ask her to think about her own wounded collision with Jesus. Invite her to think about what Jesus freed her from. She can draw a cross, she can draw a picture of her colliding with Him or maybe she might feel led to just write words.
- *I want you to spend some time thinking about what we read in Matthew, and then write somewhere on your paper the things that come to your mind that Jesus freed you from when He took them on the cross. (7 minutes)*
- *Find your own little spot in the room and spend some time in prayer, expressing your gratitude to God for taking your wounds upon Himself. Gratitude can be as simple as saying, "Thanks, God." (3 minutes)*

Group (10 minutes)

Reflect

- *Does anyone want to share what stood out to them during their individual time?*

Leader (10 minutes)

Respond

- Spend time ministering to any woman whose sharing might need it. Then close in prayer by telling your group you are going to open in prayer but then you are going to be quiet to allow them time to pray aloud their gratitude to God before you close.

Section 7
Look at the Stars

Supplies needed:
Collide Bible Study Book
Bible

Leader (10 minutes)

Welcome!

- *We spent a lot of time at the end of our session last week expressing our gratitude to God. What happened this past week that you are grateful for?*

Group (15 minutes)

Read Mark 5:30b-32
Reflect

- Discuss the first 2 reflection questions on p. 87.
- JR Edwards says, *"Jesus is not content to dispatch a miracle; he wants to encounter a person."* If this is true about Jesus, what does that tell you about Him?

Partner (10 minutes)

Reflect

- *Split into groups of 2 or 3 and use the reflection questions on p. 88 as a guide to discuss the difference between seeking God for what He can do for us versus engaging in a relationship with Him.*

Group (25 minutes)

Ruminate

- Read the verses on p. 89 out loud that show God is personal.

Reflect

- *What does it mean to look to God with expectancy?*
- *What are some ways you have believed God to be:*
  - *Distant?*
  - *Busy?*
  - *Impersonal?*
- *What are some other beliefs you have had about God that contradict the idea of Him being personal?*
- *How does what you have been learning in this study challenge those beliefs?*
- *How are you encouraged by the story Willow shares about the woman who knew her as a child, prayed for her and later saw her give her life to Christ?*
- *What does that story tell you about God?*

Partner (10 minutes)

Reflect

- *Split into groups of 2 or 3 and use the first 4 reflection questions on p. 94 to discuss the struggles you have had believing God sees you.*

Group (10 minutes)

Reflect

- *How does hearing each other's stories about how God has shown up in both personal and powerful ways, encourage you in yours?*

Leader (10 minutes)

Respond

- Pray for each member of your group by name, calling out a specific trait in her you can encourage. (If your group is large, you may want to split in half and ask a trusted group member to lead the second group.)

Section 8
The Whole Truth

Supplies needed:
Collide Bible Study Book
Bible
Whiteboard or large piece of paper

Leader (10 minutes)

Welcome!

- *Did you experience anything this week that felt special for you, like God or someone took special note of what you needed or liked?*

Group (70 minutes)

Read Mark 5:30-34
Reflect

- *Have you ever read this part of the scripture and stopped where it says, "She told him the whole truth?" What strikes you about the idea that she told him her whole truth?*
- *How does it make you feel to consider the idea that God wants your "whole truth"?*

Ruminate

- Discuss the ways we think God cannot handle our pain, sin, anger, doubt, waywardness, and weakness from pp. 100-103.
- *Which of these do you resonate with the most and why?*
- *What are some other things you believe God can't handle?*
- *Who or what told you God can't handle these things?*
- *Which of the Scripture passages spoke to you in the places you struggle?*
- **Activity** – Write the words "God, you can handle…" on the whiteboard and encourage women to call out what God can handle as you write them down.

Reflect

- *How do you feel about the fact that Jesus responded to this woman's "whole truth" by calling her "Daughter"?*
- *How do you feel about Our God claiming you as His own...you are his daughter and He is your Father?*

Leader (10 minutes)

Respond

- *God can handle the whole truth and no matter what you wrote down, He still calls you "Daughter."*
- Ask a member of the group to close in prayer, coming before God has Father.

Section 9
A Faith That Heals

Supplies needed:
Collide Bible Study Book
Bible
Whiteboard or large piece of paper
Blank piece of paper for each woman

Leader (10 minutes)

Welcome!

- *Has reminding yourself this week that you are God's daughter changed the way you view yourself?*

Group (25 minutes)

Read Mark 5:21-34
Reflect

- *What do you find interesting about the words Jesus said to this woman, "Your faith has healed you?"*
- *What are some ways you have seen people take a passive stance in their own healing and hopes?*

Ruminate

- Discuss the ways people from the Bible participated in their own lives, hope and healing from the table on p. 113.
- Read **John 5:1-12** again. *How did the paralyzed man get stuck for so long because he was waiting for the miracle he could not participate in? And what stands out to you about a God who would show up on our scenes and say to us what He said to Him: "Do you want to get well?"*

- *Do you want to get well and if you do, what are you doing to participate in your own health and life? (For more on this topic- read this blog and the associated resources: wecollide.net/stuck/)*

Partner (10 minutes)

Ruminate

- *Split into groups of 2 or 3 and discuss the 4 reflection questions that follow the table on p. 114.*

Group (10 minutes)

Reflect

- *What is fascinating to you about the idea that the woman in Mark 5 reached out to grab hold of power before she could see it?*
- *Why do you think we are waiting to see the miracle, the good news, the answered prayer, the definitive path, the "power", before we reach out and grab hold of it?*
- **Activity** - Make two columns on the white board for "Faith is not" and "Faith is" and work together to fill in the columns.

Partner (10 minutes)

Reflect

- *Split into groups of 2 or 3 and discuss the kinds of faith we see in the bleeding woman and share which of the following you most need to lean into: 1.) showing up to hope. 2.) redefining strength. 3.) reaching out for God's power even though you can't see it.*

Individual (15 minutes)

Reflect

- **Activity** – Hand out paper to each woman and invite them to pray and ask God to give them a few practical ways they can live into the kind of faith they hope to have. Then challenge them to write down 1-3 action steps they plan to put into practice this week in order to be women who couple faith with action.

Leader (10 minutes)

Respond

- Encourage women to pray out loud for each other that they would be women who live out the kind of faith that God honors.

Section 10
Missing Power

Supplies needed:
Collide Bible Study Book
Bible
Whiteboard or large piece of paper

Leader (10 minutes)

Welcome!

- *How did your challenge to take specific action steps, to lean into the kind of faith you hope to live out, go?*

Group (20 minutes)

Reflect

- Read **Mark 5:21-43**. *Why did this woman come to Jesus?*
- **Activity** – Invite women to come up and make a list of what they have heard of Jesus' power on the whiteboard with the prompt - Jesus' power...
- *As you consider the quote from Albert Einstein - "There are only two ways to live your life. One is as though nothing is a miracle. The other is as though everything is a miracle," which attitude would you say rings more true in your life?*
- *How have you seen power all around you but you haven't given it the credit it deserves?*
- *How can you relate to missing God's power as Willow shared in her stories about the plane crash, her daughter's illness and her arm injury?*

Partner (15 minutes)

Reflect

- *Split into groups of 2 or 3 and tell each other a story about a time you missed God's power because it didn't come how or when you wanted it to.*
- *Tell each other a story about a time God's power was evident in your life.*

Group (35 minutes)

Reflect

- *Share something wise that really stood out to you that your partner(s) shared regarding God and His power that you think could encourage the whole group.*
- *Discuss the reflection questions on pp.130-131.*

Leader (10 minutes)

Respond

- *Come before God together with your partner(s) and expand your prayer into these 3 areas:*

  - *God we easily miss your power- open our eyes, our faith and the ways we box you into our own expectations.*
  - *God we need your power to show up in these (circumstances in our lives).*
  - *God help us to reach for your power even when we cant see it, trusting it's there.*

Section 11
Faith or Fear?

Supplies needed:
Collide Bible Study Book
Bible

Leader (10 minutes)

Welcome!

- *What everyday miracles did you notice all around you this week?*

Group (35 minutes)

Read Mark 5:33-36
Reflect

- *How are you impacted by the statement, "Because Jesus stopped for this one woman, it cost Jairus' daughter her life?"*
- Discuss the reflection questions on p. 135.
- *Share how the voice of Fear and the voice of Faith collide in your life.*
- *Which voice tends to be louder for you? Why do you think that is?*

Partner (10 minutes)

Reflect

- *Split into groups of 2 or 3 and discuss how our negative circumstances tend to weaken our faith. Use the reflection questions on p. 141 as your guide.*

Group (25 minutes)

Reflect

- *Can you share an experience in your life that as you look back, you now see was part of a greater story?*
- *Can you share an experience where part of someone else's story played a part in your story?*
- *How might the story in **Mark 5** have been different if the bleeding woman had stayed home?*
- *Viktor E. Frankl, in <u>Man's Search for Meaning</u> said, "Everything can be taken from a man but one thing: the last of the human freedoms—to choose one's attitude in any given set of circumstances, to choose one's own way." How do you feel about the idea that God has actually empowered you with the ability to choose?*
- *Jesus gave Jairus the freedom to choose- and He even gave him advice and encouragement to choose faith rather than fear- in a sense saying it will be worth it. How do you feel about the idea that God is looking at your current circumstance that has the great ability to produce fear in your life and He sees it, He sees every angle and every layer and He says, "Don't be afraid, just believe."?*

Leader (10 minutes)

Respond

- Pray out loud together the prayer on p. 144.

Section 12
The Story's Not Over

Supplies needed:
Collide Bible Study Book
Bible

Leader (10 minutes)

Welcome!

- *What was the relationship like between your fear and faith this week?*

Group (70 minutes)

Read Mark 5:35-43
Reflect

- *As you imagine this scene that Jesus is walking into, what do you picture?*
- *In what areas of your life are you living as though the story is already over?*
- *How was Jairus living like the story was already over?*
- *Do you think Jairus chose belief or fear?*
- *How do you think Jairus would describe this entire collision with Jesus?*
- *What do you think this resurrection did for the entire community of onlookers watching?*
- *How did God use the bleeding woman to impact all those watching this miracle unfold?*

Ruminate

- Read the following truths over women asking them to listen for which truth they need to hold onto most right now in their lives.

  - *The tomb is not the end of the story*
  - *Suffering is not the final chapter.*
  - *Jesus was not only resurrected, He Himself is our resurrection.*
  - *By the same power Jesus was raised, you and I will be raised.*
  - *The story is not over and so we have a living hope.*
  - *Death no longer has mastery over Jesus and death no longer has mastery over you.*

- *Choose which truth you want to hold onto and for those who would like to share: Share "I need to hold onto this truth as I face (share circumstance you need this truth for)"*

Reflect

- *How have you forgotten that you are a "resurrection people", people who buy in, with all they've got, that with Jesus the story is never over?*
- *How are you encouraged that with Jesus you can always count on more so you can always hope?*
- *In light of all we have been discussing, what does it mean to you to be a woman of faith?*
- *Where have you seen God show up to you in personal or powerful ways throughout this study?*

Leader (10 minutes)

Respond

- Stand together in a circle, holding hands (if people are comfortable with that) and pray to the God who is Power, Resurrection and our Living Hope.

come
collide.
with us

We have more ways you

can collide with Jesus at

wecollide.net or find us on

Acknowledgements

This project was a collective work of some amazing women getting together and trusting God could use the sum of what we have to do something big. I am so very grateful for these women who poured out their energy, leaned into their giftings, gave of their time, and made great sacrifices to craft this project and get it into the hands of those we believe it will impact. God calls His people the Body, and as I like to say, God gave Collide one hot body! These beautiful women are the hands and feet, the heart and mind, the lungs and mouthpiece being used to bless the world around them and for that, I am truly grateful. There is nothing greater than together handing God what we have and seeing what He can do!

Willow

Willow Weston, Author *Willow's life is full of crazy, unexpected, broken and beautiful moments that have given way to incredible healing both in her own life and now others. Willow is a sassy, fun, word nerd. She is a spelling bee winner and an eternal 7th grader and is totally fine with it. Willow collided with Jesus and He radically changed her life and now lives to tell everyone else about Him. Willow lives in Bellingham, Washington with her husband of twenty years and her two amazing kiddos. She speaks about God's love at camps, retreats, churches, and other gatherings, in addition to her work as Founder and Director of Collide.*

Michelle Holladay, Content Contributor *Michelle believes passionately in God's word and loves helping others discover how relevant the Bible is to our everyday lives. Her ideal day would be spent on a warm beach with a good book. One day, she blinked and her two children were grown, but being a mom will always be her favorite job, one she has happily shared with her husband of over 25 years. We are so grateful for Michelle's love of God's word that guided her to help shape, research and edit the writing and content portion of this study.*

Lindsey Kiniry, Graphic Designer *Lindsey is a rodeo wrangler, a taxi driver, a chaos manager, and a really terrible chef all rolled into one most days. Though she might seem like the life of the party, this secretly shy gal loves to connect with people one-on-one in a quiet space. Lindsey has a husband, 3 kids, 2 cats, a dog and 8 chickens. Her most favorite moments are in creating something and handing Jesus the paint brush. And boy are we glad that Lindsey does because God continues to use her gifts and did so to create the art in this study that so beautifully draws us into Him.*

Anna Kuttel, Project Manager *Anna seeks to be authentic by entering into others' joy, hurt, and mess. Anna's background is composed of such seemingly paradoxical passions and experiences as anthropology and interior design, real estate and nonprofit, all of which have shaped her into a continually learning-and-growing wife, a mom of two strong and joyful young boys, and a Collide staff extraordinaire. We are ever thankful to Anna for the way she thinks, organizes, administrates and keeps us all in line- this project needed her gifts to make dreams become reality!*